PASSENGER STEAMERS

≈ *of the* ≈

GLASGOW &
SOUTH WESTERN
RAILWAY

≈ ROY WILSON ≈

The Neptune at Ayr Harbour. *Photo: Annan, Glasgow; Richard Clammer collection.*

Front cover: Glen Sannox. *G. E. Langmuir collection.*

Back cover, top: The Jupiter, possibly at the ferry rock, Corrie, Isle of Arran. *The Glasgow & South Western Railway Society collection.*

Back cover, bottom: The Neptune. *G. E. Langmuir collection.*

British Library Cataloguing-in-Publication Data
Wilson, Roy E.
Passenger Steamers of the Glasgow & South
    Western Railway
1. Passengers. Shipping
I. Title 387.
 542 09414 1

TWELVEHEADS PRESS

First published 1991 by Twelveheads Press, Chy Mengleth, Twelveheads, Truro, Cornwall TR4 8SN.

ISBN 0 906294 24 X.

PREFACE
THE GLASGOW AND SOUTH WESTERN RAILWAY

ON 28 OCTOBER 1850, by fusion of certain railway companies previously operating, there was constituted the Glasgow & South Western Railway. Never in the forefront of publicity in the railway world of its time, the G&SWR was rather an unknown quantity to the railway enthusiast of England, or even of eastern Scotland. Today, it is to many but a meaningless title.

In several ways it was an unusual railway. Its territory was not the country-wide one of the Caledonian Railway or the North British Railway. Tucked compactly into the corner of Scotland so aptly described by its title, it served that corner, undisturbed save by certain tentative intrusions by the thrustfull Caledonian. Tucked away so neatly, in fact, it was thereby somewhat overlooked by the tourist, hurrying North to the more publicised Highlands. In thus serving a well-defined corner of Britain, the G&SWR was not of course unique. The Great Eastern Railway, the South Eastern & Chatham Railway, the Great North of Scotland Railway were all examples of such railway parochialism. But these lines might be said to be more predominantly passenger carrying. Their freight traffic was chiefly of a pastoral nature. The G&SWR had these characteristics, but it had in addition that of a heavy mineral traffic, largely to and from shipping ports. These railways handled no long-distance through passenger traffic, whereas the G&SWR was partner with the Midland Railway of England for the operation of one of the two direct London-Glasgow routes.

The territory of the G&SWR was compact, and its route mileage, given in *The Railway Year Book* for 1915 as 491¾, was not particularly impressive. Among the twenty-nine companies of Great Britain and Ireland each then operating over 100 miles of route, the G&SWR took a humble seventeenth place.

The Stephenson Locomotive Society, Oct 1950

The Clyde at Broomielaw, 1900. *Photo: Annan, Glasgow.*

INTRODUCTION

IN THE VERY early years of the nineteenth century, sailing craft enjoyed the monopoly of transport on the river and on the Firth of Clyde. Not only was Glasgow developing and expanding, but the populations of the villages and hamlets on both banks of the river were on the increase. The scattered communities on the shores of the sea lochs on the north bank of the Firth and further afield in the Kyles of Bute and Loch Fyne were entirely dependent on the trade maintained by scattered groups of sailing vessels.

The islands of Cumbrae, Bute and Arran were served indifferently by a variety of sailing craft, as indeed were the isolated villages and communities on the shores of Kintyre, but trading and communications were, of necessity, limited. It was not until Henry Bell's *Comet* of 1812 and the great surge of steamboat building which followed, that the great changes came about in mass travel on the river and the Firth.

The history of these exciting and stirring times has been well documented by a variety of authors and historians. This book sets out to cover the part played by the passenger steamers of the Glasgow and South Western Railway in the final stages of independent railway ownership, leading up to the amalgamation of the railways on 1st January, 1923, and thereafter during London Midland & Scottish Railway and Caledonian Steam Packet ownership.

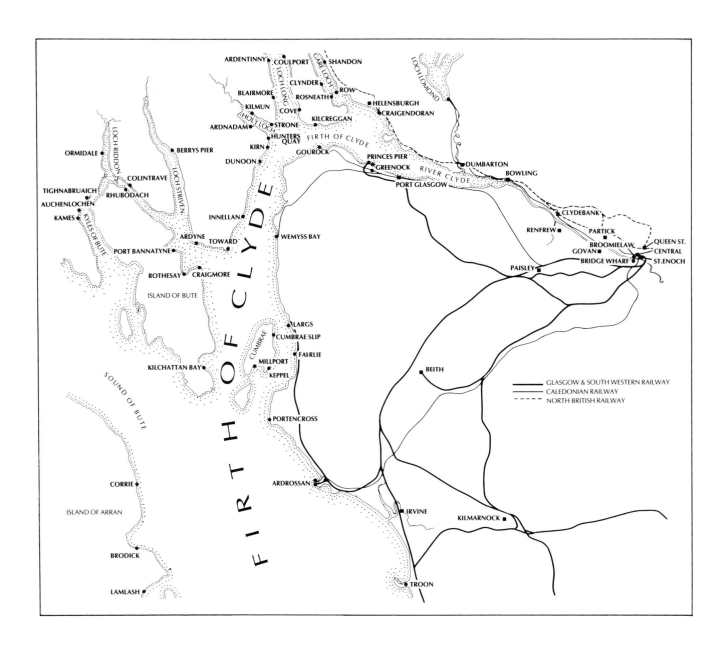

ARDENTINNY • COULPORT • SHANDON
COULPORT GARE LOCH
CLYNDER
BLAIRMORE ROSNEATH ROW
KILMUN COVE HELENSBURGH
ARDNADAM STRONE CRAIGENDORAN
HUNTERS KILCREGGAN
QUAY
ORMIDALE BERRYS PIER KIRN FIRTH OF CLYDE LOCH LOMOND
DUNOON GOUROCK
COLINTRAVE PRINCES PIER DUMBARTON
TIGHNABRUAICH GREENOCK BOWLING
AUCHENLOCHEN RHUBODACH PORT GLASGOW RIVER CLYDE
KAMES INNELLAN CLYDEBANK
RENFREW PARTICK
ARDYNE TOWARD WEMYSS BAY QUEEN ST.
PORT BANNATYNE BROOMIELAW
GOVAN CENTRAL
ROTHESAY CRAIGMORE BRIDGE WHARF ST.ENOCH
ISLAND OF BUTE PAISLEY

FIRTH OF CLYDE

LARGS
CUMBRAE SLIP
FAIRLIE
BEITH
KILCHATTAN BAY MILLPORT
CUMBRAE
KEPPEL

SOUND OF BUTE

PORTENCROSS

CORRIE

GLASGOW & SOUTH WESTERN RAILWAY
ISLAND OF ARRAN CALEDONIAN RAILWAY
NORTH BRITISH RAILWAY

ARDROSSAN
BRODICK IRVINE
KILMARNOCK

LAMLASH

TROON

LOCH RIDDON
LOCH STRIVEN
LOCH LONG
HOLY LOCH
KYLES OF BUTE

CHAPTER ONE
THE PASSENGERS

THE QUESTION HAS been asked – 'Who were all those people who wanted to, or indeed, needed to travel on the Clyde Steamers; where were they going, and why was there such a demand?'

To anyone living in that region of the country in the late 1800s the question would have seemed superfluous, indeed, almost naive, since whilst many would have had difficulty in explaining just why, all knew in their hearts the reasons why it had to be. The question, therefore, has to be addressed.

First of all, it is necessary to understand the geography of the region, to examine the terrain and to know something of the social-economic climate prevailing in the latter part of the nineteenth century. Our map of the region shows clearly the twenty-three mile stretch of the River Clyde from the centre of Glasgow at the Broomielaw (the normal extent of navigation) through the flat lands on either bank of the river to Greenock. At this point the river is flowing from east to west and the backdrop within a few miles of Greenock is of a magnificent mountain range extending, it would seem, as far as the eye can see. The scene is dramatic and the situation is dramatic; the lowlands have given way to the highlands, not gradually, but positively. The river begins to widen, although still shallow, and within four or five miles of Greenock has reached the deep waters of the Firth of Clyde, to turn gently to the south not far beyond Gourock, through the upper Firth of Clyde and thence south to the much wider lower Firth.

On the south bank are the low rolling hills of Renfrewshire and Ayrshire and the townships dotted down the dairy farming slopes to the Firth, but to the north lies a wild and mountainous country frequently indented by deep fiord-like sea-lochs running north from the Firth, starting opposite Greenock with the Gareloch and quickly followed by Loch Long and Loch Goil, then the brief but beautiful Holy Loch, followed by the steep and impressive Cowal slopes leading to the Kyles of Bute, Loch Striven and Loch Riddon.

The crofters on the north bank in the middle of the nineteenth century spoke mainly Gaelic and struggled hard to earn a living from the lower slopes of the mountains, supplemented by some fishing. Only some thirty miles away the city of Glasgow was growing and expanding at a rate which the City Fathers of the day were having the utmost difficulty in keeping under control. The areas to the south and east of Glasgow were rich in mineral resources and both coal and iron ore were being exploited to the extreme.

The need for cheap labour in the mines, the iron works and the mills was at its greatest and the highlanders, driven from their crofts by the infamous and notorious

Highland Clearances, in so far as not forced to go overseas, moved down into the city, desperate for work at any price. The tenements they became housed in, the extreme squalor and poverty in which they lived and died was to become the Glasgow of the industrial revolution, the wealthiest and yet the most squalid city of Great Britain. The second city it was called, second only to London, with its rapidly increasing industry, its heavy engineering works, its shipyards on both banks of the river, absorbing into the city all the little towns which had grown up around it into one massive conglomerate immersed in the uncontrolled sprawl of the industrial revolution.

It was inevitable that the rich became richer and the poor became poorer, and the rich, simply because they had the wealth, moved out of the city to the west to build for themselves in peaceful and beautiful surroundings, large and in many cases sumptuous homes on the banks of the Firth of Clyde and its surrounds. These then became the commuters whose demands for river travel to and from their new homes to their city offices had to be met by the steam-boat operators.

What then of the not so rich, of the working classes and of the poorer classes? It was always their wish, indeed, their utmost desire in so many cases, to get away from the dirt and squalor of their surroundings in the centre of the

Jamaica Bridge, 1905. Central Station is just off the picture to the left. St Enoch Station – headquarters of the G&SWR – is prominent on the skyline to the right. *Photo: Annan, Glasgow.*

city to those distant mountains on one of the many steam boats which they knew sailed every day from the Broomielaw to those seemingly distant parts.

By scrimping and saving up just a few shillings from hard-earned wages it was possible, now and again, to get away, if but briefly, from the filth, the grime, the smell and the noise and clamour of industrial Glasgow. For those people a shade better off came the opportunity of a week or perhaps two weeks during the Glasgow Fair Holidays in July of each year to escape to one of the Firth of Clyde sea-side resorts. Travelling there was again accomplished by steam-boat 'doon the watter'.

It should not be forgotten that the Victorians were great tourists and great excursionists, and the attraction of a day out on the Firth of Clyde was very much to the taste of the middle classes, who from Easter onwards, were to be found availing themselves of the extensive range of sailings offered by the steam-boat operators from a variety of piers and resorts on the Firth, or all the way from the Broomielaw itself.

Glasgow Central Station (Caledonian Railway) on Fair Saturday.
Photo: Annan, Glasgow.

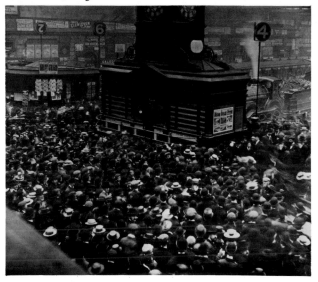

To complete the answer to the original question it is necessary to look much further afield. During the mid-1800s and thereafter, the rich and the privileged had acquired over the years vast areas of lands in the highlands and built hunting lodges and mansion houses, shooting lodges and castles, for the summer entertainment of their families and their guests.

The new absentee landlords and owners came mainly from the industrial cities of the north of England, from the Midlands and from London itself, and when they and their households, and their servants came north for the summer exodus, it was by rail to Glasgow they came.

Onward transmission was, of course, by river steam-boat and by what came to be known as the Royal Route, through the Firth of Clyde, the Kyles of Bute, Loch Fyne and by way of the Crinan Canal to Oban and Fort William, and thence through the Caledonian Canal to Inverness.

The establishment of the railheads at Craigendoran (Helensburgh), Greenock, Gourock, Wemyss Bay, Fairlie and Ardrossan, by the three railway companies, the North British, the Caledonian and the Glasgow & South Western did much to encourage commuter travel and by the 1890s a substantial weekday traffic had been built up between Glasgow and the coast. Fast steamer services, morning and later afternoon from all the piers on the north bank of the Firth to the railheads, coupled with express trains to and from the three main line stations in Glasgow, allowed an ever increasing number of business men to live on the coast but without excessive travelling time to reach their city offices.

These then were the people, these then were the passengers who for a wide variety of reasons travelled on the Clyde river steamers.

The *Iona* in the background, the *Benmore* alongside and the *Daniel Adamson* leaving the pier. Broomielaw, Glasgow, 1895. *Photo: Annan, Glasgow.*

CHAPTER TWO
RAILWAY OWNED STEAMBOATS

THE G&SWR WAS the last of the three railway companies on the Clyde to become steamboat owners and operators, and it would be fair to say that circumstances conspired to force them into this situation.

Both the North British and the predecessors of the Caledonian; the Glasgow, Paisley & Greenock Railway, made attempts to become steamboat operators in the early days and both had had failures, which in the case of the GP&GR, had resulted in complete withdrawal from steamboat operation and in the case of the North British, reduced them to a one-ship operation at the end of 1866.

The independent steamboat operators had, since the beginning in 1812, sailed from the Broomielaw to all the piers on the river and the Firth, and had the virtual monopoly of carrying both goods and passenger traffic. When the railways started to push down both the south and the north banks of the river, this monopoly was broken and for the first time, the steamboat operators had an additional and unwelcome form of competition to contend with.

The railways attracted traffic away from the river and much of the passenger traffic which took to rail travel had, of course, traditionally used the steamboats all the way from Glasgow. Now the travelling public had the alternative of rail to Greenock or to Helensburgh and thence by boat to their ultimate destination. Slightly more expensive but, of course, faster and avoiding the evil smells of the upper reaches of the river, which in the mid-eighties was virtually an open sewer.

Not that the railways were without their disadvantages on both sides of the river. The GP&GR terminus was at Bridge Street and not particularly convenient, and at the Greenock end terminated in Cathcart Street, leaving an unpleasant walk through the particularly odoriferous East Quay Lane to Custom House Quay to join the steamboats.

In the case of the North British, there was the slow and tedious climb up through the tunnel from Glasgow Queen Street Station to Cowlairs, which was cable assisted at that time, with the line going by way of Maryhill to Dalmuir and Bowling and on to Dumbarton. There was also the problem of single-line working through Dalreoch tunnel before the line terminated at Helensburgh, followed by the walk to Helensburgh pier. The North British put forward proposals for a new line along the waterfront with a railhead at or near Helensburgh pier. These proposals brought forth such a storm of protest from the good citizens of the town that no-one was surprised when the plans were ignominiously rejected. The company had, however, foreseen the possibility of this scheme foundering and as early as 1873, had sought parliamentary powers for a deviation to Craigendoran where a new railhead terminus was projected. Although work began in

Greenock Station at Albert Harbour c. 1870s. Later named Princess Pier Station. *The Glasgow & South Western Railway Society collection.*

The original Steamboat Quay at Greenock. *The Glasgow & South Western Railway Society collection.*

1880, it was the spring of 1882 before the new railhead was ready for use. Craigendoran was, however, to suffer throughout its existence from the fact that it was built in shoal waters, thus restricting for all time the draught of vessels using this pier. This fact alone was to influence in later years the design of North British ships and confine them to shallow draft paddle steamers capable of taking the ground in the drying harbour.

It had been with considerable foresight that the Greenock and Ayrshire Railway, a protégé of the G&SWR, had sought and obtained the necessary parliamentary powers to build a new line from Johnstone to Greenock via Bridge of Weir and Kilmacolm and thence through a tunnel to a new railhead at Albert Harbour, later to become known as Princes Pier. The new line was opened in December 1869 and ostensibly built to connect Kilmarnock and other Ayrshire towns with the upper Clyde coast. The Caledonian Railway apparently failed to note that the provision of a short connection from Elderlie Junction to the new line provided a direct route from Glasgow to Greenock in competition with their coast routes both to Greenock and to the Wemyss Bay railhead. Within a few years, the Sou'west opened its magnificent new Glasgow Terminus, St Enoch's Station, with trains running from the new terminus to Greenock Princes Pier, and as a consequence, eventually attracted the bulk of the

St Enoch Station, Glasgow. c. 1900. *Photo: Annan, Glasgow.*

The *Cumbrae. G. E. Langmuir collection.*

Clyde traffic to the new line. By the end of the decade they had established far and away the most popular route to the Clyde coast, except for direct Millport and Rothesay traffic via Wemyss Bay.

There seems little doubt that the directors of the G&SWR would have been quite happy with the *status quo* at their three railheads with Captain Alexander Williamson's 'Turkish Fleet', as it was known, working in conjunction with trains from St Enoch to Greenock Princes Pier and connecting with these services to Dunoon, Innellan, Rothesay and Kyles of Bute.

The railhead at Fairlie was reasonably well served by Hill & Co using the somewhat elderly *Cumbrae*, whilst the Arran connection from Ardrossan Winton Pier, was operated by Captain Buchanan's *Scotia* on an all the year round basis.

On the North Bank of the river the North British Railway had the North British Steam Packet Co. to operate their fleet of steamers from Craigendoran with services to Gareloch Piers, the Holy Loch, Arrochar excursions in connection with the Loch Lomond steamers, and a service to Dunoon, Innellan and Rothesay.

Capt. Hugh McCallum and group aboard the *Cumbrae* at Fairlie. *G. E. Langmuir collection.*

The *Scotia,* as built, leaving Ardrossan. *G. E. Langmuir collection.*

It was the completion of the highly expensive three and a half miles of railway through tunnels and cuttings to the brand new railhead at Gourock for the Caledonian Railway which triggered off what was to become the most costly and ruinous competition the steamboat operators had ever known since the inception of steamboat services on the Clyde.

The directors of the Caledonian Railway were so indignant and incensed at the luke-warm reception given to their Gourock railhead and what they regarded as the failure of the independent steamboat operators to provide services in connection with their proposed rail services from Central Station, that they finally took the momentous decision to operate their own steamer services.

They had, however, underestimated the strength and the power of the opposition to their plans and as a consequence, failed to obtain the necessary parliamentary sanctions needed if the Caledonian Railway could own and operate its own vessels. They were, therefore, compelled to resort to forming a separate company, thus overcoming the need to seek parliamentary agreement to their proposals.

In June 1889, the Caledonian Steam Packet Co. Ltd. was formed, with, as its Marine Superintendent, the very able and highly experienced Captain James Williamson.

STEAMER

SCOTIA

Captain Buchanan.

WEDNESDAY, 26th MAY, 1880.

Menu.

LUNCHEON.

Cold Roast.   Cold Corned Beef,   Hot Potatoes.
Sardines.   Biscuits and Cheese.

DINNER.

Fish.
Salmon.

Joints.
Roast Beef.   Corned Beef.   Roast Lamb.
Chicken and Ham.

Sweets.
Custard and Apple Tart.

Cheese.   Salad.

Dessert.

G. E. Langmuir collection.

CHAPTER THREE
CALEDONIAN SUPREMACY

TO APPRECIATE THE impact made on standards in steamboat operation by the arrival of this newcomer, it is necessary to pause and reflect on existing services prior to 1889. In an intensely class-ridden society, standards amongst paddle steamers varied enormously. The working people of Glasgow and the greater Glasgow area traditionally joined steamers at the Broomielaw for the 'doon the watter' exodus at the Glasgow Fair holiday and at other holidays, weekend trips and evening excursions.

Fares were remarkably low and highly competitive which, in turn, reflected on the spartan conditions on board. The steamers themselves had, of necessity, to pay their way and accordingly had been built to a strict budget price and were kept in service very often until they were fit only for the breaker's yard. All along, the least expensive form of construction had dominated specifications for new tonnage and over the years as newer forms of machinery came into vogue, so operators sought less expensive engines and boilers.

By the 1880s, the single-diagonal engine with surface condenser and low pressure hay-stack boiler had become the choice for most of the owners building new tonnage on the river. For the North British, this form of propulsion seemed adequate for the short distance pier to pier work it was programmed to carry out.

On the other hand, for the up-market owners with their beautifully appointed steamers, it seemed safer and more acceptable to their passengers to stay with older, if less efficient forms of propulsion. And so it was that David MacBrayne's mighty *Columba* had been built in 1879, using oscillating engines similar to the machinery of her elder sister of 1864, the *Iona*. A combination of long distance sailing and passenger comfort had dictated the need for an older and more expensive type of engine to suit these requirements.

The fact was that the single cylinder diagonal engine, at speed, produced a surging effect which some passengers found objectionable and which over any great period of time could be unpleasant.

The *Iona* in Rothesay Bay. *Alan Kittridge collection.*

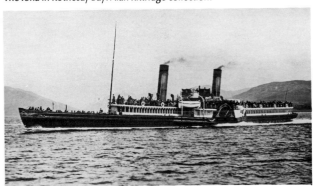

The *Lord of the Isles. Roy Wilson collection.*

The Glasgow and Inveraray Steamboat Company operated yet another of the upper-class steamboats from the Broomielaw to Inveraray, its famous *Lord of the Isles*, partly in competition with David MacBrayne, whose *Columba* and *Iona* terminated at Ardrishaig. This latter vessel, like MacBrayne's two luxurious steamers, was powered by the already obsolescent simple oscillating machinery (but diagonal, with one crank) almost certainly in the interests of passenger comfort. These large and opulent steamboats were strictly 'Butterfly boats', sailing only for the four summer months and carrying the wealthy landowners and their many guests from the Broomielaw to shooting lodges and estates in the Highlands.

Certain in their own minds that the Parliamentary Committee considering the Caledonian Railway (Steam Vessels) Bill in March 1889 would give it the go-ahead, the Caledonian Directors had pre-empted the decision of the Committee and resolved both to order new tonnage and to purchase second-hand steamboats for operation in conjunction with train services to Gourock Pier.

Captain James Williamson wasted no time in carrying out the instructions of his directors and had set about acquiring tonnage as early as December 1888.

It had, by this time, become clear to the Campbells of Kilmun that they would be extremely vulnerable to many of the services provided from Gourock Pier in the future, the family having operated steamers from Glasgow to the Holy Loch piers in the face of strong competition for many years. Accepting the inevitable, therefore, the Campbells sold their two Holy Loch steamboats, together with the goodwill of the route, to certain directors of the Caledonian and moved south from the Clyde to the Bristol Channel, there to establish in later years the magnificent fleet of P. & A. Campbell Ltd. on the Bristol Channel and South Coast waters.

The two steamers acquired, were transferred to the Steam Packet Company after its incorporation, the larger of these the *Meg Merrilies* came in an already modernised form, having been extensively renovated only the previous year, and appeared in April 1889 in the new and spectacular livery adopted for the Caledonian Steam Packet Company, calling at the new pier on her way from Glasgow to Kilmun.

In the due course of time, the second and smaller of the two former Campbell steamers, the *Madge Wildfire*, was given the same lavish treatment as her sister, where no expense was spared to bring her up to a level, both in terms of comfort and smartness, which would meet the very high standards which the new company had set for itself.

During the previous year, and no doubt in anticipation of the necessary parliamentary powers being granted, the Caledonian Railway had gone to Caird & Co. of Greenock and John Reid & Co. of Port Glasgow for two new vessels. The specifications for which had never been seen before, other than for MacBrayne's *Iona* and *Columba* or for the two *Lord of the Isles*, (which it will be remembered were designed for the luxury Loch Fyne traffic), and *Ivanhoe* for the Arran via the more select Kyles trade.

Since by April 1889 the two new paddle-steamers had not yet been completed, it was decided to charter the *Ivanhoe* from a syndicate of which Captain James Williamson was not only a partner, but had indeed been her master formerly, and it was from his *Ivanhoe* days that these very high standards in comfort and smartness had evolved. By the subtle use of pastel shades, white paddle-boxes with gold ornamentation, teak deck-houses and double gold lines around the navy-blue hull and with yellow funnels, the new Caledonian livery had been established. The crew of the *Ivanhoe* had also worn yacht-crew uniforms and this practice was extended to the Caledonian steamers.

So confident were the Caledonian Railway directors of the success of their new enterprise that they had Dugald Drummond, the company's locomotive superintendent, build for them at the Caledonian works at St Rollox, three

The *Galatea. G. E. Langmuir collection.*

more of his small-wheeled 4-4-0 express locomotives, together with three trains of ten carriages each with accommodation for both first and third class passengers, all in anticipation of greatly increased traffic to and from the coast.

By 10 June 1889 the first of the two new steamers, *Caledonia*, entered service, being placed on the Gourock – Rothesay route, thus relieving *Ivanhoe* for the Arran excursion traffic. The new steamer had been launched on 6 May and had delighted both her builders and her owners

by attaining a speed of 16.75 knots over the measured mile. Her machinery and boilers represented a complete break from the traditional hay-stack boiler and single-cylinder simple engine. Navy boilers were introduced, working under forced draught conditions in an enclosed stokehold, whilst her engines although still working on a single crank were compounded using two cylinders in tandem. This arrangement was clearly much more expensive in terms of capital cost, but it was expected that reduction in fuel costs would justify the decision.

The second steamer, the *Galatea* was launched at the end of May and entered service shortly afterwards as flag ship of the new Caledonian fleet. With a length of 230 feet she was 30 feet longer than her smaller sister and was now the largest steamer in the fleet, attaining a speed of 17.36 knots during her trials. She was the first compound twin-crank Clyde steamer ever to be built and was fitted with four navy boilers working under forced draught the uptakes being led into two funnels fore and aft of the bridge across the paddle-boxes. As the crack steamer of the day, she was placed on a daily cruise around Bute, but carrying out routine railway connections during mornings, late afternoons and evenings.

The confidence of the directors of the Caledonian Railway had not been misplaced. Their new and expensive enterprise was an instant success. The Gourock route captured the imagination of the travelling public and it came clear by the end of the Glasgow Fair holidays that their venture had exceeded all expectations. Not only was MacBrayne's *Columba* and the *Lord of the Isles* calling at Gourock Pier, but also the Belfast daylight sailing, operated from Greenock and Gourock in 1889, being transferred to Ardrossan in the following year. Trains for connection with these various steamboats were being sent off from Glasgow Central running in two and even three portions and as the *Glasgow Herald* reported 'some idea may thus be formed of the enormous number of passengers who journeyed on Glasgow Fair Saturday over the Caledonian Gourock line'.

At a social gathering of employees of the Caledonian Steam Packet Company at Gourock early in 1890, Captain James Williamson was able to demonstrate beyond any shadow of a doubt the overwhelming success of the new line, when he stated that in the period from 1 June to 31 December 1889, nearly 700,000 passengers had been carried over the new Gourock railway. The enormous success of the new line was at the expense of all the other operators. The steamer services from the Broomielaw suffered considerably and many of the small one-steamboat operators simply went out of business or by merging services managed to survive. The North British Steam Packet Company did not escape unscathed, but because of its Gareloch, Loch Long and Loch Goil operations, was not too badly affected. The Glasgow and South Western Railway with its routes via Princes Pier, took the brunt of the onslaught when traffic fell away dramatically to a level far below anything which was now economically viable.

By 1890 it became clear that worse was still to come. During the late 1880s a protégé of the Caledonian Railway, the Lanarkshire & Ayrshire Railway, had sought and obtained powers to construct a line from Lugton on the Glasgow, Barrhead and Kilmarnock Joint Railway to Ardrossan Harbour via Kilwinning, Stevenston and Saltcoats, for the main purpose of carrying coal from the Lanarkshire pits to the coast for export to Ireland. This new line would run very close to the existing Glasgow and South Western line, but would enter Ardrossan Harbour on the north side where a new pier was proposed. The Caledonian Steam Packet Co, flushed with its success on the upper Firth, now cast its eye on the Arran traffic and saw the opportunity to compete with its old rival for a share of the lucrative commuter and holiday traffic to and from the island. The G&SWR, it will be remembered, had an arrangement with Captain Buchanan who operated his paddle-steamer *Scotia* in connection with Sou'west trains to Glasgow St Enoch, with a service from Whiting Bay, Lamlash and Brodick to Ardrossan Winton Pier.

It appears that by October 1889, the directors of The Caledonian Steam Packet Co. Ltd. had formulated their plans for a new steamer, and with the approval of their Chairman, the Marquis of Breadalbane, entered into negotiation with the Caledonian Railway for the provision of a service to Arran from Glasgow Central Station.

Captain Williamson was instructed to draw up specifications for the new steamer and to invite tenders from five shipyards. It is a matter of pure speculation that at least one of these yards, Messrs A. & J. Inglis, was frightened off by the specification of a steamer 250 feet in length with compound diagonal twin-crank engines using three navy boilers with forced draught; a far cry indeed from the smaller single cylinder simple diagonal engined steamers with low-pressure hay-stack boilers which they regularly built for the North British Steam Packet Co. Be that as it may, Inglis outpriced themselves at £37,000 and Denny Bros. of Dumbarton secured the order at £24,400 for a vessel of 17 knots with a premium of £3,000 for each one knot speed in excess of 17 knots.

Work on the new steamer was pushed ahead rapidly and permission was obtained to name her the *Duchess of Hamilton*. By 10 April 1890 she was launched and ready to receive her boilers and machinery. She ran her trials on 29 May 1890 and attained a mean speed of 18.1 knots between the Cloch and Cumbrae Lights, thus winning for her builders the £3,000 premium.

Captain Buchanan's twin-funnelled *Scotia* was no match for the new *Duchess* and although he fought

The *Duchess of Hamilton. Roy Wilson collection.*

bravely to retain at least some of the Arran traffic both for himself and the G&SWR the writing was on the wall. It was now possible to travel from Brodick to Glasgow Central Station in 90 minutes and never had the travelling public enjoyed a faster and, indeed, more luxurious connection with the city. Thus, the Arran service was lavish to an extent that it exceeded the needs of the traffic to and from the island, but once again it was a boost to the determination of the Caledonian to monopolise the rail and steamer services on the south bank of the Firth.

The final nail in the coffin of the Sou'west was yet to come when the Caledonian Railway succeeded in purchasing the Wemyss Bay Railway from a difficult Board of Directors and a mediocre management, which had always given them problems in their operation of the line. The railway company's first action was to run all future services from Glasgow Central rather than Bridge Street Station, which was inconvenient to the majority of passengers using this route. In April of 1890, Captain Alexander Campbell gave notice to the Caledonian that it was his intention to withdraw his fleet of steamers from the Wemyss Bay station on the grounds that the Gourock route had taken away so much of his traffic as to make the operation of this route uneconomical. Captain James Williamson of the CSPC seems, however, to have been undeterred, since with sufficient tonnage available and two new steamers under construction, he was able to cover the Rothesay, Millport and Kilchattan Bay service without any difficulty. By the end of May the two new steamers, the *Marchioness of Breadalbane* and the *Marchioness of Bute* were in service and the Caledonian Steam Packet Co. looked as though it had achieved its objective in monopolising the rail and steamer services on the south bank of the Firth of Clyde, being firmly entrenched at its three railheads of Gourock, Wemyss Bay and Ardrossan. The fortunes of the G&SWR, as far as coastal traffic and steamer services were concerned, were now at their lowest ebb.

CHAPTER FOUR
SOU'WEST DOMINATION

IT IS TO the credit of the Board of Directors of the G&SWR that far from conceding defeat, they fought back. They had been greatly encouraged by the almost universal support of their shareholders led by the ship owner Sir J. G. Burns, when takeovers were attempted both by the North British and the Caledonian Railway, both of which were successfully fought off, and their resolve to recover a share of the coastal traffic led them to seek the necessary parliamentary sanction to operate their own steamboat fleet. They were well aware of the considerable opposition they would undoubtedly encounter and accordingly took great pains to present a petition backed by massive support from the most influential authorities and individuals they could muster. They had, after all, in a matter of only two years lost two-thirds of their coastal traffic to the Caledonian Railway and the Caledonian Steam Packet Company which had had a truly devastating effect on their coastal revenue.

It was, therefore, with the utmost care that the Glasgow and South Western Railway (Steam Vessels) Bill was drawn up with every attempt being made to avoid opposition from David MacBrayne and the operators of the *Lord of the Isles* by stating that the Sou'west had no intention of steamer calls to Tarbert, Ardrishaig or Inveraray, nor indeed to the west of Arran and to Campbeltown.

The opposition, however, was massive and included all those owners and operators the Sou'west had attempted to pacify, but to no avail. Claims and counter-claims were made, but eventually to the delight of the Board of Directors on 3 July 1891 the Select Committee of the House of Commons unanimously found the preamble to the Bill proved, with restrictions on operation east of Greenock and west of Arran. On 5 August the Glasgow and South Western Railway (Steam Vessels) Act 1891 was placed in the Statute Book.

It will be recalled that Captain Alexander Williamson had operated his Turkish Fleet comprising the *Sultan*, *Sultana* and *Viceroy*, together with the *Marquis of Bute* in conjunction with rail connections from Princes Pier,

The *Sultan* in Williamson colours. *G. E. Langmuir collection.*

The Turkish Fleet, from left to right: the *Viceroy, Sultan* and the *Sultana* at Port Bannatyne, Isle of Bute.
The Glasgow & South Western Railway Society collection.

Greenock. Following the collapse of that traffic, the Sou'west had been obliged to subsidise the routes operated by the Williamson fleet at considerable expense to themselves, simply in order to stay in business. At the Ardrossan Station, Captain Buchanan's *Scotia*, totally outclassed by the *Duchess of Hamilton*, caused him to give notice of withdrawal and here again subsidies had to be provided in order to maintain the Ardrossan – Arran service.

The Sou'west Board wasted no time in putting its house in order and by late July 1891, it had purchased the *Scotia*

operating on the Arran run and the *Chancellor* operating from Greenock on the Loch Long route to Arrochar. Arrangements were also made for the assignation of the Arran mail contract to the railway company. By 25 August 1891, the directors had appointed a Marine Superintendent, none other than Captain Alexander Williamson (Junior), the younger brother of the Marine Superintendent of the Caledonian Steam Packet Company.

This remarkable appointment caught the imagination of the travelling public and the resulting correspondence

The *Sultana* in Williamson colours. *G. E. Langmuir collection.*

The *Viceroy* as built, in Williamson colours. *G. E. Langmuir collection.*

in the *Glasgow Herald* fuelled all kinds of speculation on the fortunes of the competing fleets.

Captain Alexander Williamson (Senior) promptly sold out his fleet to the Sou'west and his son, the newly appointed Marine Superintendent, previously assistant to his father, had little difficulty in putting together a comprehensive report on the condition of the stop-gap fleet to his Board of Directors, together with recommendations for new tonnage.

By the end of September 1891 the Board had given approval to the purchase of two new vessels and had agreed to considerable reconstruction of a number of the stop-gap fleet. Of these, the *Viceroy* was the most modern of the ships thus acquired and having been extensively refitted in the spring of 1891, was ready for immediate service without further work needing to be done on her. The *Sultana* and the *Marquis of Bute* were both somewhat outdated but still capable of a good turn of speed and being favourites of the travelling public, were to be retained for a few more years. The elderly *Sultan* dating back to the early '60s was the veteran of the fleet and was to be the first ship to be disposed of following the arrival of new tonnage.

The *Chancellor* on the other hand, which had been built in 1880 for work on the Loch Long route, lent herself to extensive refurbishing and at the hands of her new owners underwent considerable alterations to improve her.

The Sou'west broke new barriers with its magnificent livery of French grey hulls, white saloons and white paddle-boxes heavily lined in gold, and red funnels with black tops. The result was magnificent, giving the

The *Marquis of Bute* at Auchenlochan, in Williamson livery. *G. E. Langmuir collection.*

The *Viceroy,* off Gourock, in G&SWR colours, with fore and aft saloons fitted. *The Glasgow & South Western Railway Society collection.*

The *Marquis of Bute* in G&SWR colours. *The Glasgow & South Western Railway Society collection.*

The *Chancellor. G. E. Langmuir collection.*

The *Chancellor. The Glasgow & South Western Railway Society collection.*

steamers, even the oldest of them, a distinctive and delightful appearance never to be surpassed, and setting the seal on a new fleet whose sheer opulence was to become the envy of the Firth.

At the end of September 1891 specifications and drawings for two new steamers had been submitted to Captain Alexander Williamson by Robert Morton, the distinguished naval architect, and it was agreed that tenders should be invited for a steamer for the Arran service and a smaller steamer for the Rothesay service with the option of a second steamer for the Rothesay service deferred for the time being. By 13 October, the Steam Vessels Committee had agreed that contracts should be placed with J. & G. Thomson of Clydebank for a steamer for the Arran service, and David Rowan & Son for a smaller steamer for the Rothesay route, but by the end of the month it had been agreed that a further contract should be placed with David Rowan for a duplicate of the smaller steamer for the Rothesay station.

The *Sultana* in G&SWR livery. *The Glasgow & South Western Railway Society collection.*

The *Scotia* in G&SWR livery. *The Glasgow & South Western Railway Society collection.*

The *Marquis of Bute* at Fairlie. *The Glasgow & South Western Railway Society collection.*

There was no room for failure and the Marine Superintendent was well aware of the fact that his job was on the line unless he had got it right. No risks were taken nor was there any question of experimentation. Morton's designs for well-proven steamers already built and successfully operating on the Bristol Channel had been selected and Morton himself employed to supervise the building of the new vessels. No expense was spared on boilers and machinery and accordingly navy type boilers with forced draught, together with twin crank compound diagonal engines were chosen for the new ships. Conditions were strict and a guaranteed speed of 17.45 knots had to be attained over a four hour period of steaming around the Firth with two double runs over the measured mile at Skelmorlie to ensure these speeds were being maintained. With an overall length of just over 220 feet the twin sisters being built by Napier, Shanks & Bell under sub-contract from David Rowan & Son were intended not only for railway connection work but also for extensive cruising and charters on both the upper and lower Firth and should they attain the guaranteed speed they would become the swiftest steamers of their size on the Clyde.

The sisters were to be named *Neptune* and *Mercury* and on 10 March 1892 the former was launched and only eighteen days later ran her trials on the Firth. To the delight, and no doubt to the relief of her builders, her designer and, of course, her owners, the new ship attained a mean speed of 18 knots and was promptly hailed as the fastest paddle steamer of her size afloat. The

Glasgow Herald waxed lyrical about the new ship, praising the accommodation and the decorations of both saloons and dining rooms as being to the highest standard of any steamer on the Clyde.

Her owners wasted no time and by 13 April 1892 the new steamer *Neptune* had been despatched to Ardrossan to relieve the stalwart, but hard-pressed *Scotia* on the Arran route. Now at last the *Duchess of Hamilton* had a worthy rival, every bit as well appointed and every bit as fast, and no longer could the Caledonian steamer leave Brodick pier five minutes after her old adversary and still be first into Ardrossan harbour.

The two rival ships were well matched and inevitably racing ensued, which, although frowned upon officially, in private was, of course, encouraged or simply ignored.

The *Neptune* as built. *G. E. Langmuir collection.*

Passenger reaction varied with only the more nervous complaining about this behaviour, but with many of the regular commuters revelling in the fact that their journey time was being reduced to and from the city. The correspondence columns of the *Herald* carried complaints about the danger to the public resulting from racing, but this was countered by letters of praise for the improved service as a result of this keen competition.

The *Scotia*, thus relieved of its impossible task, was taken up river for a much needed overhaul and re-boilering and emerged again as stand-by steamer for the Arran route and as excursion steamer on a variety of cruises.

By the beginning of May an express train leaving at 9.05 am from St Enoch Station reached Ardrossan Winton Pier in 45 minutes and per paddle-steamer *Neptune* passengers arrived at Brodick pier at 10.40 am. A 95-minute service had been established, but even shorter times were yet to come.

The *Neptune* at the coaling berth, Albert Harbour. *The Glasgow & South Western Railway Society collection.*

The *Neptune* approaching Rothesay. *G. E. Langmuir collection.*

Glen Sannox off Brodick. *The Glasgow & South Western Railway Society collection.*

The steamer ordered from the yard of J. & G. Thomson which had been designed specifically for the Arran summer traffic was launched on 26 March 1892. She was given the name *Glen Sannox* and was substantially larger than any of the existing Sou'west fleet. At 250 feet overall with twin funnels, twin-crank diagonal compound machinery of massive proportions and forced draught navy-type boilers, she was intended as the flag ship of the G&SWR. The designer, Robert Morton and the builder had, indeed, turned out an absolute masterpiece, the first ever Clyde steamer to have the plating carried up forrard to promenade deck level. Aesthetically, she was beyond any doubt the most beautiful ship on the Firth, surpassing even MacBrayne's magnificent *Columba* and the equally superb *Lord of the Isles*. She was perfectly proportioned and in the distinctive livery of her owners was to become the darling of the Arran travelling public and, indeed, to go down in history as one of the greatest paddle-steamers of all time.

The *Glen Sannox* went on trial on 1 June 1892 and amazed everyone by her astonishing turn of speed. She attained 19.5 knots average over two runs on the measured mile, actually touching 20.25 knots on one run, probably helped by both wind and tide in her favour. This incredible performance for a paddle-steamer was, however, not without its cost, since her coal consumption was very considerable, but in 1892 with a plentiful supply of cheap coal, fuel consumption was of little consequence. Although probably unaware of it at the time, Robert Morton had, in fact, reached the limits of steam paddle-boat design and within less than a decade a revolutionary new form of propulsion would take over.

The Caledonian *Duchess of Hamilton* was no match for the magnificent *Glen Sannox* and after 6th June when she took up her station on the Arran run, timings were accelerated first of all to an 88 minute connection with St Enoch, but finally on the 8.05 am run from Brodick, the **daily service to Glasgow was reduced to just 80 minutes.**

The *Glen Sannox*. The *Glasgow & South Western Railway Society* collection.

The after saloon of the *Glen Sannox. Scottish Records Office. Courtesy Richard Clammer.*

The *Glen Sannox* at moorings . *National Maritime Museum.*

Never before, nor indeed since, have the residents of Arran enjoyed such a lavish service.

Meanwhile, on 18 April 1892 *Mercury*, the second of the two smaller sisters, was launched from the yard of Napier, Shanks & Bell of Yoker, to whom the construction of the hull had been sub-contracted by David Rowan & Son, a common enough arrangement by many of the shipyards on the Clyde in these days. The new steamer ran her trials on 18 May and astonished everyone by attaining a mean speed of 18.45 knots, nearly half a knot faster than her twin *Neptune*. Whilst the two ships were at that time identical the *Mercury* for some strange reason drew one inch less than her sister at 9 feet 2 inches, which difference however hardly seems to account for the increase in speed.

With three fast modern steamers the G&SWR was now in a position to anticipate a considerable recovery in its fortunes during the summer season of 1892. Of the six second-hand steamers acquired in 1891, four had been extensively overhauled and modernised, two, in fact, being re-boilered. A comprehensive programme of excursions and cruises had been arranged in addition to faster services from St Enoch's to the three railheads at Greenock, Fairlie and Ardrossan.

In addition to this, new rolling stock had been ordered from the Metropolitan Railway Carriage & Wagon Co. of Birmingham for the St Enoch Princes Pier route. They were the first bogie vehicles to be used on these services and comprised first-class, third-class and composite first and third carriages and were welcomed by the press as

The *Glen Sannox*. G. E. Langmuir collection.

The *Mercury. G. E. Langmuir collection.*

being luxurious and handsomely decorated throughout.

Regrettably, the company appeared to have overlooked the pulling power of its locomotives which were quite simply not up to the increased weight of the new trains. It must be remembered that unlike the Caledonian riverside route, the Sou'west route ran into the Renfrewshire hills and virtually from Cart Junction at Johnstone the climb began. With a stop at Houston Crosslee for Brookfield, then the stiff climb to Bridge of Weir, thence to Kilmacolm and then to Upper Port Glasgow before the sometimes hair-raising descent through Lynedoch station and the smoke filled tunnels to Princes Pier. The little Smellie 4-4-0s were being asked to do more than they could cope with. One correspondent to the *Glasgow Herald* suggested double-heading the express trains for the difficult climb from Cart junction, but his plea went unanswered for the Sou'west, unlike its English contemporary, apparently never subscribed to the Midland Railway answer to all steep banking problems of simply double-heading anything that looked like causing delays.

Despite these complaints, however, it was clear that traffic was pouring back to the G&SWR.

G&SWR No. 128, Smellie 119 class, 4-4-0, at St Enoch Station in 1894. *The Glasgow & South Western Railway Society collection.*

The *Mercury*, departing, and John Williamson's *Benmore* at Rothesay. *Photo: Annan, Glasgow; Richard Clammer collection.*

The *Viceroy* at Cove Pier. *G. E. Langmuir collection.*

The *Marquis of Bute* alongside the Caledonian Railway's *Marchioness of Bute* at Kilchattan Bay Pier, on the Isle of Bute. *G. E. Langmuir collection.*

The *Mercury* at Hunters Quay, at the entrance to Holy Loch. *G. E. Langmuir collection.*

The *Mercury* at Craigmore, Isle of Bute. *G. E. Langmuir collection.*

The *Neptune* at Dunoon. *G. E. Langmuir collection.*

The *Neptune* and the North British Railway's *Marmion* (outside), at Arrochar, Loch Long. *The Glasgow & South Western Railway Society collection.*

The *Mercury* about to disembark passengers. *G. E. Langmuir collection.*

The *Viceroy* departing from Rothesay. *G. E. Langmuir collection.*

Princes Pier with Albert Harbour on the right. *G. E. Langmuir collection.*

CHAPTER FIVE
RUINOUS COMPETITION

THE G&SWR HAD, without doubt, won the battle to attract the public back to their route, but at a cost they could ill afford. They had won this battle, but they did not win the war. For those shareholders who attended the half-yearly meeting in Glasgow on 13 September 1892 there was nothing other than evasive answers to questions put to the Chairman, Sir William Renny Watson, and his Board of Directors.

A correspondent to the *Glasgow Herald* at that time suggested that revenue from the steamer traffic represented only one-third of the costs of maintaining the service and whilst, alas, there is no evidence to support this claim, it cannot have been too far removed from the true financial situation. There is, however, evidence to the effect that this ruinous competition was of much concern to the Caledonian: in a minute of its 13 September 1892 meeting, with a proposal that the Ardrossan – Arran winter service be worked for alternate periods by the two companies. The G&SWR rejected this proposal and came up with a counter-proposal concerning recognition of Caledonian tickets and to carry their passengers on receipt of the steamboat portion of the through fares. Agreement could not be reached and this counter-proposal was, in turn, rejected by the Caledonian.

So desperate, however, was the situation, that both companies agreed to withdraw one steamer each in the ensuing season and to honour each other's tickets between Glasgow, Paisley and the coast. Sadly, this small concession had little or no effect since severe competition once again flared up in 1893, sparked off no doubt by the heavy spending by the Sou'west on new and improved facilities at Greenock Princes Pier which, of course, had been anticipated since May of 1892 when the Company was reported to have acquired additional land alongside the site of the original station.

Princes Pier. *The Glasgow & South Western Railway Society collection.*

The *Chancellor* at Princes Pier. *The Glasgow & South Western Railway Society collection.*

The *Minerva* at Princes Pier. *The Glasgow & South Western Railway Society collection.*

At a cost of some £42,000 for the ground and proposed alterations to the station estimated to cost £20,750, recommendations were submitted to the Board for approval of this expenditure which was agreed, and after lengthy and disruptive work all was completed by the spring of 1894. On Friday, 25 May 1894, a special train carrying VIPs left Glasgow St Enoch Station for an inspection of the new station and pier buildings. The new expanded terminus rather nearer the pier itself was, indeed, a most imposing edifice. Only the Caledonian's Wemyss Bay Terminal of 1903 would ever surpass Princes Pier for sheer elegance and it has to be remembered that it was the Sou'west who led the way. The new construction had six Italianate red brick towers in front of the verandah roofs of its platforms, of which one of the larger centre towers was a clock tower. Since the trains arrived above pier level there were two long sweeping carriageways down to pier level with flights of stairs and luggage lifts connecting pier and station. Magnificent as it was, it was too large and it came too late!

As early as 11 October 1892, the Steam Vessels Committee were reviewing the subject of additional tonnage for the next season and were considering designs for a vessel of 200 feet length as proposed by Messrs J. & G. Thomson Ltd. It was decided to sell the elderly *Scotia* and to place orders for two new steamers with Thomsons, in line with the designs submitted. In the event of failure to sell the *Scotia*, only one new steamer would be built. Orders were placed for two new boats in time for the 1893 season but it was not before mid-September that the old vessel was finally disposed of. Once again, Robert Morton had been retained to supervise the construction of the new steamers and on 12 April the minutes recorded the signing of a formal contract for the purchase of the new steamers, to be named *Minerva* and *Glen Rosa*. The sister ships had been designed for winter sailings from Ardrossan and for summer excursions on the outer waters of the Firth and accordingly were of exceptionally robust construction, featuring something unique as far as Clyde steamers were concerned. In both steamers, the deck at

The *Minerva*. The Glasgow & South Western Railway Society collection.

the bow was raised to the level of the main rail and an open rail fitted above it, thus reducing the risk of flooding in heavy seas. By 6 May 1893 *Minerva* was launched and Robert Morton was able to advise the Board that the builders hoped to deliver the new vessel by 1 June.

Although rather smaller than either *Neptune* or *Mercury*, both new ships gave a good account of themselves at their trials which took place within a month of each other, with *Glen Rosa* achieving 17.75 knots over the measured mile. Once again, Captain Alexander Williamson had specified compound diagonal engines of conventional pattern with steam supplied by a double-ended forced draught boiler whose uptakes led into a single well-raked funnel. Continuing Sou'west tradition, the bridge was abaft the funnel between the paddle-boxes, and situated on the combined ticket office and Captain's cabin on the promenade deck. The *Glasgow Herald* waxed eloquent on the furnishings and fittings of the two new ships, declaring them to be luxurious and exceptionally comfortable and well up to the high standards the company had set for itself.

On 1 July 1893 came a further extravagance when *Glen Rosa* as the additional Saturday boat for the convenience of 'Families removing to Arran' sailed from Ardrossan in

The *Glen Rosa*. The Glasgow & South Western Railway Society collection.

Greenock, Custom House Quay with the *Glen Rosa* arriving. *G. E. Langmuir collection.*

The *Minerva* in Rothesay Bay. *G. E. Langmuir collection.*

G&SWR 336 class "Greenock Bogie" No. 362 at Greenock Shed yard.
The Glasgow & South Western Railway Society collection.

G&SWR train passing Elderslie on the fast line.
The Glasgow & South Western Railway Society collection.

connection with the 12.35 train from St Enoch calling at Corrie, Brodick, Lamlash, Kings Cross and Whiting Bay. This additional sailing was aimed at the holiday traffic where large quantities of luggage could be anticipated and would, therefore, be a slow run, but released the *Glen Sannox* for the normal fast service when 'No luggage will be conveyed'.

The *Scotia* was finally auctioned off on 13 September, to Mr Frederick Edwards of Cardiff at a sum of £5,300 for service on the Bristol Channel, whilst much earlier in that year, in April in fact, the old *Sultan* had been disposed of to Captain John Williamson, youngest of the three Williamson brothers, who had set up in business on his own account, for the sum of £500! Nepotism no doubt, but a modest start destined to lead to a remarkable future by the end of the century.

By the summer of 1893 competition between the Caledonian and the G&SWR had reached a new intensity out of all proportion to the increasingly heavy costs the rival companies were having to meet and more alarmingly risks were being taken which might well have led to considerable loss of life, both ashore and afloat.

Although the small-wheeled Smellie 4-4-0s were still used on the Princes Pier express train, they were gradually being replaced by No 8 class Manson large wheeled 4-4-0s, first introduced in 1892 and caused some alarm amongst passengers, who considered speeds down through the tunnels to the pier station to be excessive and dangerous. Various passengers in letters to the *Glasgow Herald* tried to draw official attention to what was regarded as reckless driving, but there is no evidence to indicate that any action was taken to improve the situation. Nor does it

The *Minerva* at Cove. *The Glasgow & South Western Railway Society collection.*

The *Minerva* and the Caledonian's *Meg Merrilies* racing towards Dunoon Pier. *The Glasgow & South Western Railway Society collection.*

seem likely that anything would have happened since the rush to get on board the steamers from the train was all a part of the race to the final destination with competing steamers sailing at full speed to be first in at the next pier. Since most intermediate piers could accommodate only one steamer at a time, the unsuccessful rival had no recourse other than to await the departure of the winner who would have picked up any passengers there might have been, before she, in turn, could come alongside. Racing for piers was not, of course, confined to railway steamers, since almost all operators of Clyde steamers had at one time or other indulged in it, and whilst officially it was frowned upon, secretly it was encouraged. Appearances before the Marine Police Court in Glasgow by various steamer Captains were not infrequent and the £5 fines imposed had little or no effect; indeed, until the ruinous competition ceased and sanity returned to the steamboat operators and to the Firth, racing would continue to be a hazard passengers had to contend with. In his book on Clyde steamers written in 1904, Captain James Williamson says:

'Throughout all seasons of the year, but especially between June and September, the rivalry between the boats of the two companies was maintained at white heat. In 1893 indeed the display of recklessness on the part of Captains had the effect of checking to some extent the popularity of the coast as a summer resort and it is doubtful if the lost ground was recovered during the decade.'

In 1895, following a lull in building new tonnage by either of the south bank railways, a new addition to the Caledonian fleet was launched from the yard of J & G Thomson of Clydebank on Saturday, 20 April. The new steamer was named *Duchess of Rothesay* which is the main Scottish title of the consort of the heir of the throne, and at that time, was held by the Princess of Wales, later to become Queen Alexandra. The new ship turned out to be a winner on all counts, having attained a speed of 18 knots

on her trials and being fitted out even more lavishly than any of her predecessors, but it was her near perfect proportions and graceful lines that aroused the greatest comment when she came into service.

Ever since 1890 it had been the policy of the Caledonian Steam Packet Company to place the navigating bridge forward of the funnel unlike the other two companies, the North British and the Sou'west, who stuck to the traditional practice of placing the bridge abaft the funnel and between the paddle-boxes. It was this feature, which in due course would be adopted by all the companies, and which helped make the new *Duchess of Rothesay* such a truly handsome ship.

Upon the appearance of this vessel, the South Western and the Caledonian concluded an armistice of five years. Some degree of sanity had returned at last, which would ultimately put a stop to the ruinous competition into which the two rivals had so recklessly entered back in the '80s and which, had it been allowed to continue, would almost certainly have had the most disastrous results.

Inevitably the arrangements made for avoiding unnecessary competition resulted in a reduction in services and the re-timing of certain express trains from Glasgow, thus incurring slightly longer overall journey times, which in turn raised a storm of protest from indignant commuters.

The service provided by the G&SWR steamer *Neptune* from Greenock Princes Pier to Rothesay, Kyles of Bute, Corrie, Brodick and Whiting Bay was highly satisfactory and in a minute dated 10 September 1895, Captain Alexander Williamson reported to the Steam Vessels Committee that in order to deal successfully with the coastal traffic it would be necessary to build a new steamer and it was resolved that the General Manager should enter into negotiations with Messrs J. & G. Thomson for a suitable steamer at a capital cost of between £22,000 and £23,000.

On 19 November a further minute recorded that a

contract had been placed with J. & G. Thomson for the building of a new steamer, to be named *Jupiter* at a price of £23,550 to be ready for delivery on 1 May 1896. The launch took place on 21 March, but the new ship did not run her trials until 16 May. Once again, Robert Morton had been responsible for the supervision of the building of the new steamer and it may well have been that trials were delayed until he was entirely satisfied with the performance of the ship. In the event, her trials exceeded the greatest expectations of both her builders and her new owners for she averaged 18.5 knots on two runs over the measured mile at Skelmorlie and just over 18 knots on a four hour steaming trial.

With an overall length of 230 feet, fully plated up to its bows and once again powered by compound diagonal machinery, the new steamer was a larger and faster version of the Caledonian *Duchess of Rothesay* and destined to become a great favourite of the public. Steam was provided by a double-ended navy boiler under forced draught conditions, with the flue gases exhausting into a single funnel and once again the Sou'west steadfastly stuck to the traditional layout of placing the navigating bridge abaft the funnel between the paddle-boxes.

The arrival of the new steamer meant that the elderly

The *Jupiter* off Gourock. *The Glasgow & South Western Railway Society collection.*

The *Jupiter. National Maritime Museum.*

The *Jupiter*, nearest; the *Lord of the Isles*, centre;
and the *Marchioness of Bute*; at Rothesay.
Richard Clammer collection.

The *Jupiter* at Brodick Pier, with the *Glen Sannox*
behind. *Roy Wilson collection.*

The *Jupiter. G. E. Langmuir collection.*

Sultana was now surplus to requirements and the General Manager was instructed to put her up for sale. A first attempt to negotiate a sale with a Plymouth based company was unsuccessful, but in a minute dated 11 August 1896 it was reported that the old steamer had been sold to Captain John Williamson for the sum of £750. Nepotism again!

By the same year, 1896, the North British had at last two steamers which could compete with the Sou'west and the Caledonian on the Rothesay route, the *Redgauntlet* and the *Talisman*. Both could have been described as budget price steamers and both had the by now obsolescent single diagonal engine and low pressure hay-stack boiler. Despite this, however, both steamers had a good turn of speed and were just as fast as their more sophisticated Sou'west and Caledonian sisters.

The *Redgauntlet* of the North British Railway's fleet. *G. E. Langmuir collection.*

Although the G&SWR considered the building of a duplicate of the *Jupiter* in 1897 on the recommendation of their General Manager, Captain Alexander Williamson, nothing came of it despite an offer from Clydebank Shipbuilding & Engineering Co. Ltd. (successors to J. & G. Thomson) to build a new vessel for the sum of £25,000.

It appears, however, as though the Board of Directors were beginning to have second thoughts about additional tonnage because on 14 June 1898 the following Board minute was recorded:

'New Steamer: The Chairman reported that the Clydebank Shipbuilding & Engineering Co. Ltd., had offered to sell to the company a steamer 15 feet longer than the *Jupiter* which had been built for a company who had been unable to raise the purchase price, and the question of the purchase was remitted to Mr. Caird and the Chairman.'

A fortnight later on 28 June at a meeting of the Steam Vessels Committee another minute recorded:

'New Steamer: Mr Caird reported that . . . he had, along with Captain Williamson, inspected the steamer offered . . . and the result of the inspection being satisfactory, he had given instructions for the purchase of the steamer at £27,000 on condition that certain alterations which he and Captain Williamson had suggested were carried out and that the steamer be completed and ready for delivery not later than 4th proximo – the guaranteed speed to be 18.5 knots on a four hour run. It was resolved that the steamer be called the *Juno*.'

She was of a much heavier build than the average Clyde steamers of her time with a length overall of 245 feet, a beam of 29.1 feet and a moulded depth of 9.7 feet. Her machinery was just as massive as was her general appearance but for all that she was a very handsome steamer and was to become yet another great favourite of the public. By now the two-cylinder compound diagonal engine with steam supplied from a double-ended horizontal boiler had become the norm for new Sou'west tonnage and provided both the speed and comfort anticipated by the public when sailing on South Western steamers.

The *Juno* was certainly fast – she achieved a mean speed of 19.26 knots during her trials on 5 July 1898 – but alas, like her sister the flagship of the fleet *Glen Sannox*, her coal consumption was extravagant and was in the end to bring about her comparatively early demise.

The new steamer was immediately placed on the Ayr excursion station, thus releasing *Neptune* for other work further up the Firth, and was to become associated with sailings on the lower Firth for virtually the whole of her career. Her massive proportions and high speed suited her well for the more turbulent waters of the lower Firth and enabled her to cover comparatively extensive cruises in the course of a normal working day.

The turn of the century came and went, Queen Victoria had died and a new monarch was on the throne. For some time now, both builders and owners had realised that development of the paddle-steamer had reached its zenith and it came as no real surprise that a new form of propulsion in the shape of the turbine steamer would be destined to succeed.

The *Juno's* engines. *G. Stromier.*

The *Juno. G. E. Langmuir collection.*

The *Juno. The Glasgow & South Western Railway Society collection.*

The *Juno* at Lochgoilhead. The German Band, having gone ashore from the steamer, is giving a performance at the head of the loch.
G. E. Langmuir collection.

The new turbine *King Edward* proved beyond any doubt that the larger, faster ships for the long distance routes would undoubtedly be driven by turbine machinery but for pier-hopping and short distance work on the upper Firth, and on the river and inner lochs, the paddler still had a long lease of life.

By the year 1901, the Sou'west had taken the decision to dispose of the paddle-steamer *Chancellor* despite the fact that although only 21 years old she still had a great deal of life left in her. It can only be surmised that because she was one of the original six second-hand steamers acquired by the company, it was felt the time had come to replace her. She was sold to La Herculina Ferrolana, Ferrol, Spain and renamed the *Commercio* and is understood to have sailed for them until finally broken up in 1919.

To take the place of the *Chancellor* in the fleet the G&SWR added another steamer in 1902. The new steamer was built by John Brown & Co. Ltd., successors to the Clydebank Shipbuilding & Engineering Co Ltd and formerly so very well remembered as J. & G. Thomson Ltd.

John Browns had recently built for the Caledonian Steam Packet Company a new steamer named *Duchess of Montrose* and it is interesting to note how the ship ordered by the G&SWR so closely approximated to the Caledonian steamer. There were differences, of course; she was ten feet shorter than the new *Duchess* and had a slightly broader beam, being driven by a two-cylinder compound diagonal engine with steam supplied by navy boilers in a forced draught stokehold. In appearance she was a traditional Sou'west steamer with navigating bridge abaft the funnel and between the paddle-boxes, as indeed were all her elder sisters in the fleet. Like the *Montrose* she had relatively small paddle-wheels and paddle-boxes, a feature clearly influenced by the builders, making both vessels distinctively different from other steamers in either fleet, the adoption of which was never repeated in subsequent tonnage of the period. The new paddler was named *Mars* and was launched on 14 March 1902, when after satisfactory trials giving mean speeds of 16 knots had been recorded, she entered service on the Princes Pier – Rothesay, Kyles of Bute – Ormidale route in June of that year.

The activities of Captain Alexander Williamson, Marine Superintendent of the Sou'west, and his brother, Captain John Williamson, continued in the year 1904 when the old *Marquis of Bute*, of 1868 vintage and considered inadequate, was replaced on a part-exchange basis with a comparatively new steamer, the *Britannia* built originally as the *Kylemore* for John Williamson in 1897, but re-named and sold off the river by him before completion. This replacement to the fleet was promptly renamed *Vulcan* and being of modern design, similar in size to the *Minerva*, *Glen Rosa* and *Mars*, was dependable and economical to run and a considerable improvement to the *Marquis of Bute* on the all important Millport service.

In the year that followed no further tonnage was added, but by September of 1905 the Company considered the ordering of a new steamer with a view to ultimately replacing the last of the original second-hand steamers, the by now ageing *Viceroy* of 1875. It will be

The *Mars* being launched on 14 March 1902. *Scottish Records Office; Richard Clammer collection.*

The Mars fitting out at the yard of John Brown & Co. Ltd. *Scottish Records Office; Richard Clammer collection.*

The *Mars* leaving Princes Pier. *The Glasgow & South Western Railway Society collection.*

The *Mars. Roy Wilson collection.*

The *Vulcan. The Glasgow & South Western
Railway Society collection.*

The *Vulcan. G. E. Langmuir collection.*

The *Vulcan's* engines. *G. E. Langmuir collection.*

remembered that in 1901 the first turbine steamer, the *King Edward* went into service and in the following year after its instant success and tremendous popularity, came the turbine *Queen Alexandra*, even larger and faster than the *King Edward* but both owned by the same syndicate, Turbine Steamers Ltd., with none other than Captain John Williamson as its General Manager.

The Sou'west Board of Directors were no doubt well aware of the fact that in the previous month, August 1905, the Caledonian Steam Packet Company had accepted an

Turbine Steamers Ltd's *King Edward* in East Kyle. *Roy Wilson collection.*

offer by William Denny & Brothers of Dumbarton for the construction of a turbine steamer of dimensions 250 feet x 30 feet x 10.6 feet. The proposed new ship was almost identical in size to the *King Edward* and, therefore, 20 feet shorter than the *Queen Alexandra*, but having many refinements and improvements both in machinery and in passenger comforts contained in the specifications.

The *Queen Alexandra* of Turbine Steamers Ltd. *Roy Wilson collection.*

The dilemma now facing the Board of the G&SWR was that of choice of propulsion for a new steamer; turbine or reciprocating paddle-wheel machinery? Originally it had been the intention of the Company to order a repeat of the paddle-steamer *Mars* of 1902, but it appears from a minute of the Glasgow & South Western Steam Vessels Committee dated 19 September 1905, in which the Marine Superintendent was instructed to obtain alternative tenders for a turbine and a duplicate of the steamer *Mars*, that the Board had an open mind. By 17 October the Committee met again and recorded the following minute:

'New Steamer: Submitted drawings of a proposed Turbine Steamer and also a duplicate of *Mars* with certain improvements:- authority was given [by the Board] to accept the offer of John Brown & Co. Ltd. for a Turbine Steamer as per their offer of 3rd October at £21,000.'

The launch party for the G&SWR's turbine steamer, the *Atalanta*, on 23 April 1906. *Scottish Records Office; Richard Clammer collection.*

It was decided that the new steamer be called *Atalanta* and she was duly launched on Monday, 23 April 1906. Since she was intended to be a duplicate of *Mars*, she was of similar dimensions and her length was, therefore, only 210.4 feet, making her very much shorter than any of the three existing Clyde Turbine Steamers, but with a beam of 30.1 feet, she was as broad as the Caledonian *Duchess of Argyll*. She ran her trials on 12 May shortly after her launch, and appears to have satisfied her builders attaining a speed in excess of the guaranteed 17.5 knots. Clearly, it had never been the intention of the Sou'west that the new steamer was intended for the fast routes like

The *Atalanta. The Glasgow & South Western Railway Society collection.*

The *Atalanta. Roy Wilson collection.*

The Caledonian turbine, *Duchess of Argyll*. Alan Kittridge collection.

the other three turbines and she soon settled down to a variety of excursions, evening cruises and general duties. It has been suggested that her owners were not entirely satisfied with her trials performance but accepted her on condition that at the end of the season she was returned to the builders for re-boilering. She was very well fitted out internally and, in line with Sou'west policy, came up to the high standards of passenger comfort which the Company had years ago set for itself. The only break away from tradition, for the first time, and indeed as it turned out, for the last time, was the fact that the navigating bridge was placed forward of the single funnel. A small upper promenade deck was placed aft of the funnel over the purser's office and the companion way to the main deck.

Steam was supplied by two navy boilers from a forced draught stokehold feeding three direct-drive steam turbines, one high pressure and two low pressure. It is said that when John Brown offered to build the new ship, they already had a triple set of turbines of the right size which had been built to the Denny/Parsons design to give their own engine builders experience of this new type of propulsion. John Brown & Co Ltd had already obtained the order for the two Cunard liners *Carmania* and *Lusitania* both of which were to be powered by steam turbines that would be of considerably greater size. It

seems, therefore, that the *Atalanta* may have been designed around this small scale set of turbines which could account for her extreme beam in relation to her length. There have been suggestions that she was not a particularly successful steamer with a tendency to roll in heavy weather, though she is credited with having been a very good sea-boat in stormy conditions.

Apart from serving on most of the G&SWR excursion routes she was regularly on the weekly excursion to Stranraer in 1907 and the Arrochar run in 1908. She assisted on the Ardrossan – Arran route over the years, but when pooling arrangements came into operation between the Caledonian Company and the Sou'west in 1919, the *Atalanta* was one of the ships which was laid up for the entire season. She later became associated with the Arran route on a regular basis and by the LMS was employed for her final season on the Fairlie – Millport station.

By 1907 the ageing *Viceroy*, last of the second-hand steamers, had been disposed of and sold off the river and in 1908 the *Vulcan* was sold back to Captain John Williamson who promptly renamed her *Kylemore* and brought her back into up-river service.

No further tonnage was ever built by the Sou'west but by 1908 they had a splendid fleet of nine modern, beautifully appointed steamers, possibly the finest fleet the Clyde had ever known, or indeed would ever experience again.

The *Kylemore*, ex-*Vulcan*. Alan Kittridge collection.

CHAPTER SIX
WORLD WAR ONE

WHEN THE FIRST World War broke out in August 1914 to the dismay and consternation of a largely unprepared population, the River Clyde fleet of passenger steamers numbered some 40 vessels, 24 of which had been built in the 19th century and the eldest of which, the third *Iona* of 1864, was already 50 years old.

Not surprisingly she was considered by the Admiralty to be unsuitable for war service and in consequence, remained as one of the much depleted fleet to maintain a service both on the river and on the Firth. Sailing on the Ardrishaig route from Wemyss Bay, she eventually went on charter to the Caledonian Steam Packet Co. in 1916 to help maintain the all-important Rothesay connection.

Not all of the older ships, however, escaped the attention of the Admiralty, and many were to be requisitioned, modified and adapted for war service along with their younger sisters. In all, 28 of the 1914 river fleet were called up for active service, many in the role of minesweepers, since the paddle-steamer with its relatively shallow draught adapted well to this all-important war-time duty.

So pleased were the Admiralty with the performance of paddle sweepers that they placed orders for 16 paddle minesweepers to designs by the Ailsa Shipbuilding Company of Troon, all of which were to be completed between April and October of 1916.

These ships were built by yards throughout the United Kingdom, several being built at Troon and other Ayrshire yards, whilst on the river, others came from such well know builders as A. & J. Inglis of Pointhouse who built HMS Newbury, launched in July 1916, and Fleming and Ferguson of Paisley who built HMS Lingfield, launched earlier, in April 1916, both of whom were again to be involved in an even later part of the Emergency War Programme.

HMS Melton, one of the Admiralty's paddle minesweepers, built in 1916 by W. Hamilton & Co. Ltd., Port Glasgow. She later saw service as a passenger steamer in the South of England. *G. E. Langmuir collection.*

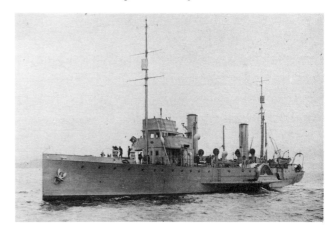

A further group of seven paddle minesweepers designed by the Admiralty, adapted from the Ailsa Shipbuilding Company's design of 1916, were completed between January and July 1918, having similar dimensions to the original 16 insofar as hull, boilers and engines were concerned, and once again, several Clyde yards were involved.

They were not unattractive ships, having two funnels well spaced before and abaft of the paddle-boxes but with the combined chart room, wheel house and bridge forward of the leading funnel. Rigged with both foremast and mainmast, carrying two spars on the foremast with short aerial spars on both masts, and fully plated up to promenade deck level, they had about them an appearance which could not belie their purpose.

Having regard to the very considerable shipping losses sustained by the allies during four years of war, it seems in retrospect somewhat surprising that of 28 Clyde river steamers requisitioned for war service, only five were, in fact, lost due to enemy action.

The first of these ships to fall victim to the enemy has been described as 'one of the most beautiful and best known of the Caledonian steamers' – the first *Duchess of Hamilton*. Being both a fast and powerful paddle- steamer, built as she had been by William Denny & Bros. of Dumbarton for the Ardrossan – Arran run in her early years, it seemed inevitable that the Admiralty would requisition her for war service. And so it was, that in February 1915 she was drafted into naval service as a troop carrier, being well suited for the Channel crossing, but after a comparatively short period in this activity, she was adapted for the much more dangerous work of minesweeping. It was whilst thus engaged that she was blown up and sunk near the Longsand, just off Harwich on 19 November 1915.

It was to be March of 1917 before the loss of a second Clyde river steamer occurred, again due to enemy action. The *Duchess of Montrose*, yet another of the Caledonian fleet and small by comparison with her more famous sister, the *Duchess of Hamilton*, had been requisitioned by the Admiralty for troop carrying. *HMS Montrose*, as she was styled by the Navy, was subsequently transferred to minesweeping and it was whilst carrying out these duties in preparation for a British naval raid that she was blown up and sunk after hitting a mine off Dunkirk on 18 March 1917.

Her career had been relatively short-lived; in all, fifteen years, and certainly during her Caledonian days singularly unspectacular, since she had never attained the popularity with the travelling public enjoyed by her more famous *Duchess* sisters, the *Hamilton*, the *Rothesay* and the *Fife*. From the beginning she never really seemed to stand much of a chance in the popularity stakes. When new she was despatched to Ayr to carry out excursion work in competition with the G&SWR's magnificent and beautiful *Juno* by comparison with which she must have seemed but a pale shadow. She was no match for the Sou'west steamer and was eventually relegated to the more mundane general railway runs from Gourock and Wemyss Bay until called up for war service.

Tragically, within just one month of the loss of the *Montrose* came news of the sinking of *HMS Nepaulin*, first of the G&SWR steamers to fall victim to the ravages of war. When new in 1892 she was the *Neptune*, one of the two sisters built by Napier Shanks & Bell of Yoker for services from Greenock Princes Pier. In the ruinous, almost suicidal competition between the Sou'west and the Caledonian Steam Packet Co. the need by the former for two larger and faster boats to increase their share of the coastal traffic was imperative. Coming into service in April of 1892 the *Neptune* was put on the Arran – Ardrossan run, relieving Captain Buchanan's sorely pressed *Scotia* (at that time working in connection with the G&SWR), but only briefly, since shortly after completing her acceptance trials, the legendary *Glen Sannox* took over the Arran run, for which indeed she had always been intended. The

The *Isle of Cumbrae* was owned by Buchanan Steamers Ltd. She was chartered to the G&SWR between 1916-1919 for services from Princes Pier. *G. E. Langmuir collection.*

Neptune then joined her twin sister, the *Mercury*, on the Rothesay and Kyles of Bute service from Greenock to Princes Pier. Gradually over the years that followed, her appearance began to change as she was adapted and modified for excursion work in which she was now fully employed, going as far afield as Stranraer on a weekly basis during the summer months. The forward end of her fore- saloon was plated as were the forward paddle-wings, and the original rectangular windows removed and replaced by portholes, By the time both ships were requisitioned by the Admiralty, they had acquired deck-houses fitted over the saloon companionways aft and it was in this condition they went off to war. *Mercury*, although badly damaged on two occasions, survived her war, but *HMS Nepaulin* fell victim to a mine near the Dyck Light Vessel and sank on 20 April 1917.

Next of the Clyde steamers to be lost to the enemy was *Minerva*. Built by J. & G. Thomson of Clydebank in 1893 as one of a pair for the G&SWR, she was shortly after joined by her consort *Glen Rosa* from the same builders. Rather smaller than many of the paddle-steamers built for them in that period, the Company had specified ships of very sturdy construction, having in mind using them as winter service boats capable of the arduous crossings on the Ardrossan – Arran run. Although built as twins, *Minerva* differed slightly from her sister, being the more graceful of the two, largely through having a more distinctive sheer both fore and aft.

Both ships, however, had their cut-away bows plated up to bulwark level, decked over, and then railed off. The promenade deck, though well proportioned, did not extend far beyond the mast and the forrard end of the fore

HMS Minerva. G. E. Langmuir collection.

saloon had been strengthened to a considerable extent and fitted with portholes rather than the customary rectangular windows.

It came as no surprise to the Sou'west when the Admiralty requisitioned both ships and ordered them off to war. *Glen Rosa* was to survive hostilities and to give a great deal of pleasure to countless thousands of passengers in years to come, but alas for *Minerva* her days were already numbered. Sent out to the Mediterranean, where she was based at Malta as an auxiliary patrol, she had the misfortune to be captured by the Turks in 1917 whilst carrying out her duties in the Aegean Sea. After the Armistice in 1918 the Admiralty sold her to Turkish owners for Bosphorus ferry service and the little paddler never returned to the Clyde. She is believed to have survived until 1927 before being broken up.

The *Glen Rosa* as *HMS Glencross*, pictured at Ilfracombe during World War One. She was renamed to avoid confusion with P&A Campbell's Paddler, Glen Rosa, which was in the same minesweeping flotilla. *The Glasgow & South Western Railway Society collection.*

On the night of 18 November, seven days after the war had ended, the G&SWR paddle-steamer *Mars* was run down by one of our own destroyers whilst engaged in minesweeping activities in the approach to Harwich Harbour. Conscripted by the Admiralty and renamed *HMS Marsa*, the sturdy little paddler gave sterling service in the defence of the Eastern Approaches, but her back was broken in the violent collision and all attempts to salvage her failed. Built in 1902 by John Brown & Co. Ltd. of Clydebank (successors to J. & G. Thomson), the *Mars* closely resembled her elder sister *Jupiter*, but at 200 feet overall, was some 30 feet shorter in length. In keeping with the G&SWR policies of the time, she was designed for general work on the lower Firth and like both *Jupiter* and *Juno* was plated up and decked to the bow. As it transpired she was to be the very last of the Clyde fleet to be lost as the direct result of the war.

By November of 1918, with the people of Glasgow and the Clyde picking up the pieces after the appalling losses of a victorious but disastrous war, and trying desperately to rise above the tragic and broken lives with which so many of them seemed beset, the battered, tired and war-weary ships of the Clyde river fleet began to return home.

They returned to a river which had never seen such industry and productivity in its entire industrial existence; an existence during which the work of the shipyards had been prolific.

There was a great deal of tonnage still to be completed at the shipyards with much overhaul and repair work yet to be carried out. To an increasing number of men and women it became clear that the war-time boom would soon be over and the spectre of mass unemployment became an increasing threat that all too soon became a reality. The world fit for heroes, so readily promised by

HMS Mercury alongside *HMS Eagle* – Buchanan Steamers Ltd's *Eagle III. G. E. Langmuir collection.*

politicians, no longer seemed easy to visualise and to very many folk it seemed that fate was about to deal them another bitter blow.

In retrospect, it seems all the more surprising that despite the incredible hardship of the years that were to follow, the shipbuilders and the shipbuilding industry survived to fight and win another war.

For the G&SWR however, the immediate need was to have their ships refurbished as quickly as possible and to restore them to their former stations on the Firth of Clyde, but first of all to recover them from the clutches of the Admiralty, who at times seemed reluctant to part with the little ships which had seen such valiant service.

On 1 January 1919, a public notice in the *Glasgow Herald* proclaimed that:

'Notice is hereby given that all restrictions on cruising of yachts, excursion steamers, motor boats, pleasure boats etc. on the South-West and West Coast of Scotland imposed under the Defence of the Realm Regulations by competent Naval Authorities in the Coast of Scotland Command, are withdrawn as from 1st January 1919.'

The source of this communication was the office of the Coast of Scotland Commander-in-Chief at Rosyth Dockyard.

On 25 March 1919 the G&SWR received the Royal Assent for the transfer of Ayr Harbour which was formally vested in the Company in early April. Amongst many traffic requirements incorporated in the Act was an all-important provision that over the period of the next ten years the Sou'west must spend not less than £50,000 on improvements and new equipment.

Although many of the Clyde steamers requisitioned by the Admiralty at the outbreak of the war had now returned to the Clyde, it was to be 28 June 1919 before the magnificent *Juno*, the steamer so closely associated with the resort of Ayr, returned to her station to take up, once again, her lower Firth excursion traffic with which she had

been so long associated. But such was the need to cover the all-important Rothesay sailings from Greenock Princes Pier that it was, indeed, the summer of 1920 before *Juno* was firmly based at Ayr.

By the end of 1920 the somewhat reduced fleet of the G&SWR had been re-installed on the pre-war routes served by the Company, but no further tonnage was contemplated or built. During 1921 and 1922 the situation remained unchanged and it is of interest to note that not a single one of the owners on the river and the Firth placed orders for additional tonnage.

On 1 January 1923 amalgamation of the railways, or the grouping, as it is often called, took effect and the Glasgow and South Western Railway Company, together with its arch-rival, the Caledonian Railway Company, were absorbed into the London Midland and Scottish Railway (the Caledonian not until 1 July). The Caledonian Steam Packet Co. Ltd. then became a subsidiary of the LMS and so, later, of British Railways and of the Scottish Transport Group. It has been named Caledonian MacBrayne Ltd. since the transfer to it of certain ships of David MacBrayne Ltd. On 1 January the North British, together with its fleet of steamers, became part of the London and North Eastern Railway.

This rationalisation of the railway system throughout the country brought to an end the ruinous competition of previous decades (which had been largely curtailed from 1908), but for many of the travelling public the exciting and truly colourful years of the railway steamers had gone for ever.

CHAPTER SEVEN

SOU'WEST BOATS IN LMS DAYS

WHEN THE LONDON Midland and Scottish Railway was formed on 1 January 1923, it inherited a Clyde fleet of G&SWR and Caledonian steamers amounting to some twelve operational ships plus the old *Marchioness of Lorne* which, however, was no longer in commission. In addition to this was a sundry collection of tugs and dredgers stationed both on the Firth of Clyde and on the Firth of Forth.

No changes were to take place until 1924 when the Steam-boat Committee of the LMS decided to replace the *Glen Sannox* on the Ardrossan – Arran run with a more economical vessel. Excessive tonnages of around 20 tons of coal per day were making the paddler much too expensive to run.

The LMS had already in the joint fleet the former Caledonian turbine steamer *Duchess of Argyll* which had

The *Glen Rosa* in the LMS livery of 1923/4. *National Maritime Museum.*

The *Glen Sannox* at Lamlash, in LMS livery. *Roy Wilson collection.*

The *Mercury* in the early LMS livery, with the tricolour funnel. *The Glasgow & South Western Railway Society collection.*

entered service way back in May of 1906 and had proved to be both economical and fast, and had over the years become a great favourite of the travelling public.

Accordingly, on 18 June 1924 the LMS invited tenders for a vessel of similar proportions. Not surprisingly Wm. Denny & Bros. of Dumbarton submitted a proposal for a replica of the *Duchess of Argyll* which they had built in 1906, and despite the fact that 17 years had elapsed since this vessel had entered service, their offer was accepted at a price of £58,000, nearly £27,000 more than the *Argyll* had cost in 1906.

It is clear from subsequent events that they had saved themselves between £12,000 and £14,000 against a vessel of more modern design, since only one year later Turbine Steamers Ltd. ordered from the same yard a ship which was to capture the imagination of the public and which

represented the very latest in design and technology, the magnificent *King George V* which both in appearance and amenities (except that she had no proper saloon) totally outclassed the apparently obsolescent design built for the LMS.

Despite this, however, an order was placed on 6 August 1924 for a replica of the *Duchess of Argyll*, yard no. 1170, later to be given the name *Glen Sannox* as a replacement for the paddler of the same name. Dimensions and displacement were, therefore, almost identical to the earlier ship of 1906 as was the machinery comprising three shaft single reduction Parsons geared turbines with one double-ended return tube boiler, but with astern power greatly augmented as against earlier vessels of a similar type.

The *Denny List* states that the new *Glen Sannox* was

The *Juno* arriving at Rothesay. *Roy Wilson collection.*

launched on 24 February 1925 and that on her trials between the Cloch and Cumbrae Lights she attained a mean speed of 21.15 knots. She entered service in the early summer on the Ardrossan – Arran run replacing her predecessor which was sold to Smith & Co. and broken up at Port Glasgow in the same year.

In support of the choice of this nineteen year old design it has to be said no risks could be taken in providing a replacement for the paddler and, therefore, it was essential that a tried and tested design, already known to meet the requirements of this fast passenger service should be the choice. The backbone of the Arran – Ardrossan service was, in fact, the all the year round commuter traffic, used morning and late afternoon, by business men residing on Arran and travelling to and from their offices in the city of Glasgow. The middle of the day runs were utilised less frequently by other residents on the island and by farmers moving stock to the markets on the mainland. The spacious promenade deck of the ship could be penned off to provide accommodation for sheep or cattle, and to carry a limited amount of deck cargo, and also, in later years, to carry motor cars.

The LMS turbine *Glen Sannox* of 1925. *Roy Wilson collection.*

In the summer months came the great exodus of families moving to rented accommodation on the island for the long summer school holidays, often two months, and those who took their week or fortnight between June and September. This traffic, in turn, was supplemented by the day excursionists taking the steamer on the round trip from Ardrossan to Brodick and thence to Lamlash and Whiting Bay, with time ashore before making the return trip. This latter traffic was much sought after by the LMS to augment the numbers carried on regular sailings and was heavily advertised both on station bill-boards and the local press in Glasgow and surrounding towns, offering cheap day-excursion fares usually from June to September.

Neither the Sou'west *Glen Sannox* nor her LMS successor operated during the winter months when the volume of traffic fell away substantially. It will be recalled the route was maintained by the sturdy little *Glen Rosa* and somewhat later by the former G&SWR turbine *Atalanta* much to the chagrin of the daily commuters who took great exception to the re-timings of the ship which added considerably to the journey times to and from Glasgow.

In the years that followed 1925 many fine old steamers fell victims to the ravages of time and were consigned to the breaker's yard, but it was not until the end of the 1931 season that the next of the old G&SWR fleet was itself to be withdrawn from service. The paddle steamer *Juno*, second largest of the original Sou'west fleet, had been stationed at Ayr ever since 1898 and apart from service in the Great War as *HMS Junior* and a brief spell on the Princes Pier – Rothesay route in 1919, had seldom vacated her station. *Juno* was an excursion steamer and was extremely popular with the holiday-makers visiting that part of the Ayrshire coast during the summer months. When the announcement came that she was to be withdrawn from service, great regret was expressed at the passing of so fine a steamer. Like the paddle steamer *Glen Sannox* however, it was her excessive appetite for coal

The *Atalanta* in the early LMS colours.
The Glasgow & South Western Railway Society collection.

The *Mercury* with the tricolour funnel and black hull livery of 1924. *The Glasgow & South Western Railway Society collection.*

The *Juno* in the LMS colours of 1924. *The Glasgow & South Western Railway Society collection.*

The *Juno* in the livery adopted from 1925. *The Glasgow & South Western Railway Society collection.*

which was to bring about her somewhat premature demise.

Meanwhile, on 28 November 1929 the LMS had signed a contract with Wm. Denny Bros. of Dumbarton for a triple-screw excursion turbine steamer in the name of the Caledonian Steam Packet Company.

The new steamer would measure 260 feet water-line length, with a beam of 32 feet and a mean draught of 6.10 feet with 20.5 knots to be attained, and would be named *Duchess of Montrose*. Here at last was a truly modern-looking railway turbine steamer with extensive sheltered accommodation on the promenade deck, two semi-elliptical funnels instead of narrowly placed funnels (as in the turbine *Glen Sannox*), a well raked stem and a handsome cruiser stern. On her trials in August 1930 the

The *Duchess of Hamilton. Alan Kittridge collection.*

The *Duchess of Montrose. Alan Kittridge collection.*

new ship attained a speed of 20.7 knots over the measured mile and almost overnight became the darling of the travelling public. The excitement caused by the arrival of this new turbine was further enhanced by the fact that she was registered as a Caledonian Steam Packet Company steamer and, therefore, unlike an LMS steamer, was not restricted in any way to calls as far afield as Campbeltown. Her excursions covered every area of both the upper and the lower Firth and her considerable speed ensured that these visits could be comfortably covered in any one day. Being a one-class ship, she had very spacious and luxurious accommodation.

The undoubted success of this steamer prompted the LMS to go out to tender for an almost exact copy of the *Montrose* and this time, Messrs Harland & Wolff Ltd obtained the order for their Govan Yard, with machinery being built at Belfast. The new ship was named *Duchess of Hamilton* and she took the place of the *Juno* on the Ayr station running excursions from Ayr, Troon and Ardrossan during the summer of 1932 to Arran ports, Campbeltown and Stranraer with frequent circumnavigation both of Arran and Ailsa Craig. Like her sister she was registered in the name of the Caledonian Steam Packet Co. Ltd. and so could visit ports prohibited to the *Juno*.

The 1930s were, however, to see the last of the G&SWR fleet and in 1933 came the next casualty when the *Mercury*, the third Sou'west steamer of 1892 and sister ship to the ill fated *Neptune* was withdrawn from service after being on various runs from Greenock, Gourock and Wemyss Bay and she was sold in December of that year to T. W. Ward Ltd. to be broken up at Barrow.

The name, however, was to be perpetuated when in 1934 two paddle-steamers of a revolutionary design joined the LMS/CSP fleet. These quasi-sisters were named *Mercury* and *Caledonia* and were built by the Fairfield

Company and by William Denny Bros of Dumbarton respectively. Controversy raged at the appearance of these steamers on the Firth and the public were deeply divided in their opinions and impressions of this breakaway from the popular concept of the traditional Clyde paddler. Gone were the lean rakish lines so long associated with Clyde river paddle steamers to be so faithfully reproduced as recently as 1931 in the form of the legendary LNER steamer *Jeanie Deans*. Gone were the graceful swept back paddle-boxes with the customary vents which from the very beginning had been the distinguishing feature of every Clyde paddler, and finally, as though to underline this breakaway from all that had gone before, the disappearance for all time of the shapely counter-stern.

The new steamers had promenade decks plated up to the bows and running almost the entire length of the hull. The paddle-boxes were disguised to give the impression side-on of a turbine steamer and extensive deck shelters were provided, thus giving considerable upper deck space. Two masts were fitted, together with a single wide elliptical funnel and topping it all a flying bridge over the Captain's cabin on the upper deck. As far as the LMS was concerned, this then was to be the final development of the paddle steamer. The *Mercury* was transferred to the Caledonian Steam Packet Co. Ltd. in 1938, the *Caledonia* having been their's from the start.

At the end of the 1935 season in her 39th year the former G&SWR paddler *Jupiter* was withdrawn from the Wemyss Bay – Millport run on which she had sailed since 1934 and ended her career by being sold to Messrs T. W. Ward of Sheffield to be broken up at Barrow. Time was running out for the two remaining former G&SWR steamers and, in March 1937, *Atalanta*, the only turbine steamer owned by the old company, was sold to the Blackpool Steam Navigation Co. Ltd. for service out of Blackpool and Morecambe. She survived the war as a Boom Defence Vessel but was finally broken up at Methil in 1945.

The last survivor of the G&SWR fleet was the *Glen Rosa*. Built as will be recalled as a winter boat for the often

The *Jupiter. Roy Wilson collection.*

The *Jupiter* approaching Rothesay. *The Glasgow & South Western Railway Society collection.*

The *Atalanta. The Glasgow & South Western Railway Society collection.*

tempestuous passage from Ardrossan to Arran, the paddler had worked hard over the winter months and in the summer had cruised around the upper Firth on excursion work from Greenock. She had been considerably modernised in 1926.

Although often used in summer on the Cumbrae Circle and relegated in the mid-thirties to the Cumbrae trade, eventually to the Wemyss Bay – Millport run, she enjoyed a brief indian summer in the short-lived boom in Clyde excursions before the war clouds over Europe ended it all. She was the only former G&SWR steamer to become a Caledonian Steam Packet Company vessel, which she did in 1938. In 1939 she was laid up in Albert Harbour, Greenock, and in August of that year was sold to Arnott Young & Co. (Shipbreakers) Ltd. and broken up at Dalmuir.

POSTSCRIPT

The car ferries of Caledonian MacBrayne serve the waters of the Firth of Clyde and the Western Isles. The name of the Glasgow & South Western Railway Company is all but forgotten, together with the fleet of steamers which in its heyday was the fastest, the most opulent and, indeed, the finest fleet ever to grace the waters of the Firth of Clyde. The famous names of the steamers of yesteryear have, however, not been forgotten and the Cal-Mac fleet of 1989 boasted such famous names as *Juno*, *Jupiter* and *Glen Sannox*, a reminder of great years that long since have passed, along with *Saturn*, which might have been, but never was a Glasgow & South Western Railway name.

The *Atalanta. G. E. Langmuir collection.*

The *Glen Rosa*, the last G&SWR survivor in the LMS fleet, approaching Rothesay in June 1936. *G. E. Langmuir collection.*

The *Glen Rosa* at Rothesay in July 1938. *G. E. Langmuir collection.*

GLASGOW & SOUTH WESTERN RAILWAY
FLEET LIST

BUILT ACQUIRED DISPOSED	NAME	TYPE	SHIPBUILDERS & ENGINEBUILDERS	LENGTH	BREADTH FEET	DEPTH	GROSS TONS	MACHINERY	REMARKS
1861 1891 1893	SULTAN	IRON PS	BARCLAY CURLE & CO. J. BARR	176.0	16.6	7.2	124	St. 1 cyl. 45 ins. x 42 ins. ex-*WELLINGTON* b. 1853	New boiler 1877 Lengthened 1865 Original length 166 feet
1868 1891 1896	SULTANA	IRON PS	ROBERTON & CO. W. KING & CO.	188.1	18.3	7.3	198	Diagonal 1 cyl. 49 ins. x 54. ins	New boiler 1866
1868 1891 1904	MARQUIS OF BUTE	IRON PS	BARCLAY CURLE & CO.	196.6	18.1	7.3	196	Diagonal 1 cyl. 48. ins x 60. ins	New boiler 1892
1875 1891 1907	VICEROY	IRON PS	D & W HENDERSON & CO. HUTSON & CORBETT	208.9	20.1	7.1	236	Diagonal 1 cyl. 51 $\frac{1}{2}$ ins. x 60. ins	New boilers 1886 & 1897 Lengthened 1891
1880 1891 1901	CHANCELLOR	STEEL PS	R. CHAMBERS JR. BLACKWOOD & GORDON	199.7	21.1	8.2	272	(1) S. Diagonal 2 cyls. 36 ins. x 60 ins. (2) C. Diagonal 26 ins. & 48 ins. x 60 ins.	New boiler 1892 Compounded 1892
1880 1891 1893	SCOTIA	IRON PS	H. McINTYRE & CO. W. KING & CO.	211.2	21.8	8.3	260	St. 2 cyls. 45 ins. x 48 ins.	New boiler 1892
1892 1892 1917	NEPTUNE	STEEL PS	NAPIER SHANKS & BELL. D. ROWAN & SON.	220.5	26.0	9.2	378	C. Diagonal 2 cyls. 33 ins. & 62 ins. x 60 ins.	New boiler 1912
1892 1892 1925	GLEN SANNOX	STEEL PS	J & G THOMPSON LTD.	260.5	30.1	10.1	610	C. Diagonal 2 cyls. 34 $\frac{1}{2}$ ins. & 74 ins. x 60 ins.	
1892 1892 1933	MERCURY	STEEL PS	NAPIER SHANKS & BELL D. ROWAN & SON	220.5	26.0	9.2	378	C. Diagonal 2 cyls. 33 ins. & 62 ins. x 60 ins.	New boiler 1912
1893 1893 1917	MINERVA	STEEL PS	J & G THOMPSON LTD.	200.0	25.0	8.3	306	C. Diagonal 2 Cyls. 26 ins. & 55 ins. x 24 ins.	New boiler 1902
1893 1893 1939	GLEN ROSA	STEEL PS	J & G THOMPSON LTD.	200.0	25.0	8.3	306	C. Diagonal 2 cyls. 26 ins. & 55 ins. x 24 ins.	New boiler 1926 C. S. P. Co. from 1938
1896 1896 1935	JUPITER	STEEL PS	J & G THOMPSON LTD.	230.0	28.1	9.0	394	C. Diagonal 2 cyls. 30 $\frac{1}{2}$ ins. x 65 ins. x 60 ins.	
1898 1898 1932	JUNO	STEEL PS	CLYDEBANK E. & S. B. CO.	245.0	29.1	9.7	592	C. Diagonal 2 cyls. 33 ins. & 71 ins. x 60 ins.	
1902 1902 1918	MARS	STEEL PS	JOHN BROWN & CO. LTD.	200.4	26.1	8.6	317	C. Diagonal 2 cyls. 28¼ins. & 53 ins. x 54 ins.	
1897 1904 1908	VULCAN ex-BRITANNIA ex-KYLEMORE	STEEL PS	RUSSEL & CO. RANKIN & BLACKMORE	200.5	24.1	7.7	319	C. Diagonal 2 cyls. 23 $\frac{1}{2}$ ins. & 47 ins. x 51 ins.	
1906 1906 1937	ATALANTA	STEEL Tr. SS	JOHN BROWN & CO. LTD.	210.4	30.1	10.3	486	3 Steam Turbines direct drive.	New boiler 1930

SOURCES AND ACKNOWLEDGEMENTS

A PERSONAL KNOWLEDGE of the Firth of Clyde and the adjoining sea lochs, their piers and landing places, has been much augmented by a study of *Clyde Piers* by Ian McCrorie and Joy Monteith.

Much historical and topographical information was obtained from a study of C.A. Oakley's book *Second City* and the work of Colm Brogan in his book *Glasgow Story* which highlights the social and economic conditions of the period. John Riddel's illustrated history, *The Clyde*, helped me greatly in setting the scene.

The journals and other publications of the Clyde River Steamer Club over the years, and the Reviews of 1913 and 1919 have provided a wealth of valuable information which again helped me considerably in compiling this record, and I express my gratitude to all those who made this possible.

The late Cameron Somerville in his excellent publication *Colour on the Clyde* helped me to understand more about the characters and personalities of those who worked on and sailed on the steamers.

I have drawn heavily on the peerless works of Alan J. S. Patterson in his books *The Golden Years of the Clyde Steamers*, *The Victorian Summer of the Clyde Steamer* and *Classic Scottish Paddle Steamers*, and wish to express my indebtedness to him.

Iain C. MacArthur's substantial volume *The Caledonian Steam Packet Company Limited* helped and influenced me considerably as indeed did *Clyde Passenger Steamers 1812–1901*, by Captain James Williamson, both of which books contain a wealth of information.

My keen interest in Clyde passenger steamers was stimulated years ago by two books, *Clyde Steamers of Yesteryear* and *Steamers of the Clyde and Western Isles*, both books by the same authors, MacArthur, McCrorie and MacHaffie, followed shortly by *Steamers of the Clyde*, written by the late George Stromier and illustrated so well by John Nicholson.

My considerable thanks must go to Graham E. Langmuir whose *Clyde River and Other Steamers* by Duckworth and Langmuir (now in its fourth edition) has been an inspiration to me, and who kindly undertook the task of reading and editing the text of this book. Very many of the photographs contained in the book are from the Graham E. Langmuir collection, and were selected from the extensive choice of negatives made available to me. The Fleet List at the back of the book is from *Clyde River and Other Steamers*, and is reproduced by kind permission of the author.

I owe a debt of gratitude to Stuart W. Rankin, Archivist to The Glasgow and South Western Railway Association, who provided an extensive choice of photographs of steamers, piers, stations, locomotives and rolling stock, together with maps and timetables, some of which are illustrated in the book.

Further valuable railway information came from The Stephenson Locomotive Society's publication, *The Glasgow & South Western Railway Company*, and from the very informative *Regional History of the Railways of Great Britain, Volume 6*, by David St. John Thomas and Alan J. S. Paterson.

I am indebted to the Scottish Records Office, and in particular to Mr G. R. Barbour for his help in providing me with a synopsis of minutes of the Steam Vessels Committee of the Glasgow & South Western Railway, which helped me considerably in my researches.

Information on the First World War was obtained largely from *Jane's Fighting Ships*, 1919 edition and from articles appearing in contemporary editions of the *Glasgow Herald*.

The *Denny List* published by the National Maritime Museum provided valuable information, particularly of the turbine steamers built by that company.

I am indebted to Alan Kittridge for his help and encouragement and for his constructive suggestions and valuable advice during the preparation of this book.

To Mr Murdoch Nicholson of the Mitchell Library I would like to express my appreciation for his help and advice, and to Mr D. Williams, Director of Library Services, Leeds City Libraries, my thanks to both he and his staff for valuable information provided.

Finally I would like to thank my wife, Ruth, for her patience and continuous encouragement during the somewhat lengthy period it has taken to complete this work.

The *Neptune* and the *Galatea* at Rothesay. *National Maritime Museum.*

BIBLIOGRAPHY

SOURCE MATERIAL

Minute Books – The Glasgow & South Western Railway Co.

Acts of Parliament – Glasgow & South Western Railway (Steam Vessels) Act 1891.

Timetables, public notices, publicity material etc.

BOOKS AND BOOKLETS

Brogan, Colm *Glasgow Story*. Frederick Muller, London, 1952.

Brown, Alan *Craigendoran Steamers*. Aggregate Publications, Johnstone, 1979.

Clammer, Richard *Paddle Steamers 1837 to 1914*. B. T. Batsford Ltd., 1980.

Cleary, Robert *Atalanta*. Clyde River Steamer Club Publications, Glasgow.

Cox, Bernard *Pleasure Steamers*. David & Charles, 1983.

Davies, Kenneth *The Clyde Passenger Steamers*. Kyle Publications, 1980.

Duckworth & Langmuir *West Highland Steamers*. T. Stephenson & Sons Ltd., 1967.

Duckworth & Langmuir *West Coast Steamers*. T. Stephenson & Sons Ltd. 1966.

Duckworth & Langmuir *Clyde River and Other Steamers*. Brown Son & Ferguson Ltd. 4th edition, 1990.

Galbraith, Rev W. C. *The Caledonian Steam Packet Co. Ltd., The Sixtieth Anniversary of*, C.R.S.C. 1949.

Hope, Iain *The Campbells of Kilmun*. Aggregate Publications, Johnstone, 1981.

MacArthur, McCrorie & MacHaffie *Steamers of the Clyde & Western Isles*.

MacArthur, McCrorie & MacHaffie *Clyde Steamers of Yesteryear*. Motherwell, 1966.

MacArthur, Iain C. *The Caledonian Steam Packet Co. Ltd.*. Clyde River Steamer Club, Glasgow, 1971.

McCrorie, Ian *To the Coast*. The Fairlie Press, Fairlie, 1989.

McCrorie, Ian *Clyde Pleasure Steamers*. Orr Pollock & Co.Ltd., 1986.

McCrorie, Ian & Monteith, Joy *Clyde Piers*. Inverclyde District Libraries, 1982.

Oakley, C. A. *Second City*. Blackie & Son Ltd. – London & Glasgow, 1946.

Paterson, Alan J. S. *Classic Scottish Paddle Steamers*. David & Charles, 1982.

Paterson, Alan J. S. *The Golden Years of the Clyde Steamers*. David & Charles, 1969.

Paterson, Alan J. S. *The Victorian Summer of the Clyde Steamers*. David & Charles, 1972.

Riddell, John *The Clyde*. The Fairlie Press, Fairlie, 1988.

Somerville, Cameron *Colour on the Clyde*. Bute Newspapers Ltd.

The Glasgow & South Western Railway Co.. The Stephenson Locomotive Society, 1950.

Stromier, George & Nicholson, John *Steamers of the Clyde*. Scottish Field Publication.

Thomas, John & Paterson, Alan J. S. *Regional History of the Railways of Great Britain, Volume 6*. David & Charles, 1971.

Thomas, John *Steamers of the Clyde*. Ian Allan Ltd., 1948.

Williamson, Captain James *Clyde Passenger Steamers 1812- -1901*. MacLehose & Sons, 1904 (reprinted Spa Books, Stevenage 1988).

NEWSPAPERS

Glasgow Herald.

Gourock Times.

Greenock Telegraph.

PERIODICALS

Clyde Steamers (Clyde River Steamer Club).

Review 1913 (Clyde River Steamer Club).

Review 1919 (Clyde River Steamer Club).

Journal of The Glasgow & South Western Railway Association.

Paddle Wheels, Journal of the Paddle Steamer Preservation Society.

MISCELLANEOUS

Leeds City Libraries.

National Lending Library for Science & Technology, Boston Spa, Yorkshire.

National Library of Scotland, Salisbury Place, Edinburgh.

Jane's Fighting Ships, 1919, David & Charles Reprints.

Mitchell Library, Glasgow.

National Maritime Museum, Greenwich, London.

Scottish Record Office, H. M. General Register House, Edinburgh.

The Denny List, National Maritime Museum, Greenwich, London.

The *Viceroy* at Fairlie. *G. E. Langmuir collection.*

95

INDEX OF SHIPS